More great, original do-it-yourself projects
in the same series:

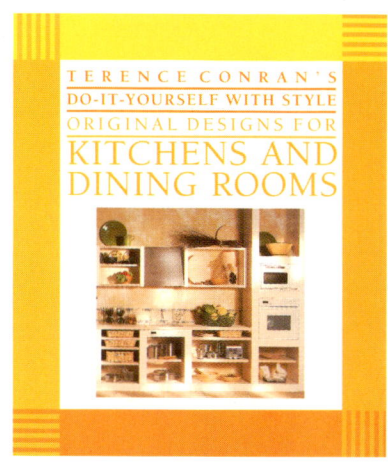

TERENCE CONRAN'S
DO-IT-YOURSELF WITH STYLE
ORIGINAL DESIGNS FOR
KITCHENS AND
DINING ROOMS

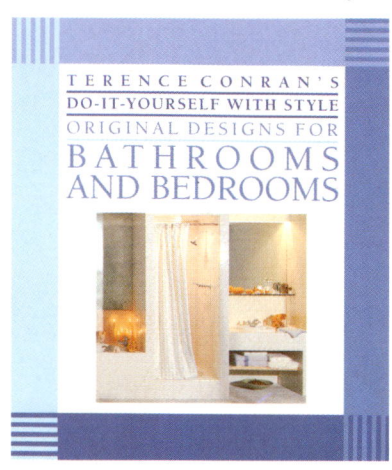

TERENCE CONRAN'S
DO-IT-YOURSELF WITH STYLE
ORIGINAL DESIGNS FOR
BATHROOMS
AND BEDROOMS

PROJECTS
The Kitchen System: Basic Units
Wall-mounted Shelf Unit
Plate Rack and Drip Tray
Knife Rack * Drying Rack
Serving and Display Unit with Mirrors
Divided Shelves
Hanging Bars
Suspended Shelves
Door Fronts

PROJECTS
Tiled Bathroom: Bathtub Unit
Shower Unit
Basin Unit
Paneled Bathroom
Towel Rod
Wardrobe with Hinged Doors
Folding Screen
Japanese Wardrobe
Bed with Trundle Drawer

TERENCE CONRAN'S
DO-IT-YOURSELF WITH STYLE
ORIGINAL DESIGNS FOR
LIVING ROOMS
AND WORK SPACES

CONSULTING EDITORS
JOHN McGOWAN AND ROGER DuBERN
PROJECT PHOTOGRAPHY BY HUGH JOHNSON

A FIRESIDE BOOK
PUBLISHED BY SIMON & SCHUSTER INC.
NEW YORK   LONDON   TORONTO   SYDNEY   TOKYO

FIRESIDE
Simon & Schuster Building
Rockefeller Center
1230 Avenue of the Americas
New York, New York 10020

First published in 1989 in Great Britain by
Conran Octopus Limited
37 Shelton Street, London WC2H 9HN

10 9 8 7 6 5 4 3 2 1

Library of Congress Cataloging in Publication Data

Conran, Terence.
    [Do-it-yourself with style]
    Terence Conran's do-it-yourself with style : original designs for
living rooms and work spaces / photography by Hugh Johnson.
        p.   cm.
    "A Fireside book."
    Includes index.
    ISBN 0-671-68719-0
    1. Living rooms.   2. Recreation rooms.   3. Interior decoration–
–Themes, motives.   I. Johnson, Hugh.   II. Title.   III. Title: Do-it
-yourself with style.
    NK2117.L5C65   1989
    643'.54--dc20   89-11611
                                                         CIP

Typeset by Servis Filmsetting Limited
Printed and bound in Italy by Amilcare Pizzi SpA

The publisher would like to thank the following companies
for supplying material for photography:

30 The Conran Shop; **39** General Plumbing Supplies;
61 Authentics, INC Office Equipment, The Conran Shop.

Project Editor JOANNA BRADSHAW
Assistant Editor SIMON WILLIS
Copy Editor RICHARD DAWES
U.S. Consultants RAY PORFILIO, MILES HERTER

Art Editor MERYL LLOYD
Design Assistant ALISON SHACKLETON
Illustrator PAUL BRYANT
Visualizer JEAN MORLEY

Photographer HUGH JOHNSON
Photographic Stylist CLAIRE LLOYD
Photographic Assistants SIMON LEE, PETER WILLETT

Picture Research NADINE BAZAR
Production SHANE LASK, SONYA SIBBONS

PUBLISHER'S ACKNOWLEDGMENTS
The publisher would like to thank the following for their
invaluable assistance in producing this book:

The Conran Studios, Julie Drake, Rebecca Verrill,
Malcolm Harold and all at Benchmark Woodworking
Limited, Tabby Riley, and Alex Wilcock.

The projects in this book were specially built by SEAN SUTCLIFFE
of Benchmark Woodworking Limited.

Special thanks to PAUL BRYANT for his superb original illustrations.

PLEASE NOTE
Before embarking on any major building work on your home,
you should check the law concerning building regulations and
planning. It is also important to obtain specialist advice
on plumbing, gas, and electricity, before attempting any
alterations to these services yourself.
    While we have made every effort to ensure that all the
information contained in this book is correct, the publisher
cannot be held responsible for any loss, damage, or injury
caused by reliance on such information.

DIMENSIONS
Do not mix imperial and metric when you are making a calculation.

Contents

INTRODUCTION

More than any other room, a living room should reflect your personal taste and way of life. It is here that your own ideas of comfort, elegance, style, and decoration can be put into practice. You can dramatically enhance the personality of the room by restoring existing features or introducing character by adding architraves, moldings, and other architectural devices. Shelves in living rooms are normally used for displaying treasures and collections, and exert a strong influence on the room. When you do-it-yourself, shelves can be custom-made to suit the room and your possessions. In addition, an ugly fireplace can be revamped, and wooden floors can be made good by stripping and waxing, staining or painting. The installation of a new lighting system can transform a room.

Workrooms and studies must be both practical and comfortable: with a little planning you can convert a small room (or even a corner of a room) into a purpose-built home office or workroom. With the right shelving, lighting, and display you can make your work area both a delightful place to be in and a truly functional space for your particular requirements.

Terence Conran.

DESIGN FOR LIVING

The living room is a place where any work you do yourself should be of the highest quality that you are capable, given time and money.

The shelving system in this comfortable cozy living room (previous page) is well finished and has been cleverly designed to fit wall-to-wall. It also runs around the room at picture-rail height, above the door. The top shelf provides a decorative display area for an attractive and imposing collection of wooden horses. Accent lighting is provided by ceiling downlighters.

DISTINCTIVE DISPLAY

Designing a display unit involves careful consideration of many factors. A fitted unit for storage and display must respond to the shape, character, and decorative scheme of the room as well as to the objects it will house. In a luxurious modern house (right) a designer has created a room of strong, clean lines in which the materials are important. The display unit for contemporary ceramics, books, a television, and a VCR, with useful drawers beneath for hidden storage, has continued this theme. Natural wood has been used for the wide shelf and as edge-banding for the upper shelves, providing graphic lines in a quality material. The positioning of the ceramic pots was of importance in the design, but equally well thought-out was the position of the television. The gray shelves and drawer fronts complement the sofa and blend beautifully with the color-washed wall behind and its striking modern painting.

In a more conventional setting (below left) low closets fill an alcove. The space above has been used creatively and lends character to the room. To provide a large area for plants and bulky objects, there is a gap above the closets and then small pigeon-holes for individual items, with a further section for books.

The equal squares formed by a simple white display unit (below right) echo the design of a glazed door. Such a design suits a collection of treasured objects which require prominent display and which are linked to one another through texture and color.

AROUND THE CORNER

The owner of this room clearly likes to work close to a collection of books. The polished floor and antique furniture ensure that the room (left) retains the atmosphere of a study rather than a home office. In keeping with this character, the custom-made black shelves fit neatly into two corners of the room and are strong and distinctive. Shelves finished in cream or white, and designed to fill rather than edge a wall, would "disappear" into the structure of the room. With this design, the shelves, and the books they contain, are given prominence. Black used so extensively can be very effective, but it has to be linked to the decorative scheme – hence the black chair seat and lampshade.

SMALL SPACES

In an open-plan studio, the kitchen is part of the living room but cleverly separated from it by a small island unit (below left). An upright radiator has been installed to save further space. Because space is limited, there is very little display in the room and the design is utterly plain and easily built by a home woodworker.

In a small awkward corner of a living room, an inventive design for shelves, an alcove, and low closets works on many levels (below right). It uses space effectively, providing neat hidden storage behind plain doors as well as open shelves for books. The alcove also provides an enhancing framed display for a plaster bust, which demands pride of place in the room. By painting the whole structure white to match the walls and avoiding decorative detailing, the unit successfully merges into the room.

ASSESSING THE WORKLOAD

Nothing can rival hand-made, custom-designed, original fixtures and features in a living room. However, this is not a room in which to experiment with your wood-working ability: the standard of work must be as high as you can make it, the quality of the materials as good as you can afford, and the detailing and finishing as perfect as your skills allow.

If, for example, you want a fully fitted closet which is going to add character to the room as well as useful storage, try building a similar structure as a trial run in a less exposed area of the house. If you want some fitted shelves for displaying a treasured collection, think carefully about the design, and, if you are not particularly confident, choose the design which is easiest to construct.

Some of the most effective tasks you can undertake in the living room will, if they are done properly, "disappear" when completed. Wire management is

one of them: remove baseboards and floorboards so that you can channel wires from lights, the television, music equipment, and so on to an area that will be hidden when you replace the woodwork. If this is not possible, box-in wires and any water pipes as necessary. Flat speaker wires can always be run under carpet.

Another effective home improvement task is to dispense with superfluous fixtures. Unwanted shelves attract clutter, so do not think that you must always add fixtures to a room; sometimes taking away unnecessary elements can be equally important and liberating.

The architectural details of a room have a subtle but important impact. By re-vamping or replacing woodwork such as architraves, dado rails, valances, paneling, baseboards, and so on you will greatly improve the appearance of the room. All of these tasks are relatively simple, but enormously effective.

INSPIRING WORK

The three rooms illustrated here have each benefited from both good design and the work of highly skilled professional craftspeople, who have created well-conceived and superbly finished work.

A broad display shelf (above left) has distinctive and strongly decorative metal supports designed to define the structure and give it, and the objects it carries, handsome prominence in the room.

In a beautifully mellow, welcoming, and elegant room (above right), the distinctive oak baseboard and the fireplace's wooden frame are absolutely made-to-measure.

Magnificent woodwork (opposite) in a Shaker room results from the skills of generations of craftsmen. The simple structures are stunning in their practical beauty. The detailing on joints, handles, and hinges has a charming quality which declares the great pleasure and care with which these fixtures were conceived and constructed.

STRUCTURAL SHELVING

Shelving that is designed specifically for the space that it fills and the objects which it displays is likely to be far better than any that you buy ready-made or in kit form. The crucial point to remember is that shelves should always blend in well with the dimensions and architecture of a room rather than stand out from them.

If you are installing shelves in an alcove, fill the alcove from top to bottom and from side to side. Never run a line of shelves down the center of an alcove, because you will create ugly gaps around it. If you are building a wall of shelves, make sure that they cover the entire wall. Where the wall is interrupted by a door, why not frame the door with the shelving structure.

When a room contains awkward spaces, such as a low or sloping attic wall, consider installing a shelving system which can make excellent use of an otherwise wasted space.

Framing shelves by lining the area to be shelved with wood at the top, bottom, and sides will give them a professional finish and a neat definition. Scribing the frame and securing it to the wall is no more difficult than installing kitchen units; the shelves themselves will then be attached to the wooden frame rather than to the wall, and brackets or supports can be incorporated into the frame. Dividers and shelves can then be made to the same specification as the frame, and act as supports for the shelves as well as giving a pigeon-hole effect.

As as general rule, it is a good idea to use a shelving system that allows brackets to be completely invisible. One of the most effective ways of achieving this is to make the shelves from hollow oblong pieces of wood rather than from single planks, so that brackets can be attached inside the structure. This method of attachment also gives the shelves a strong, sculptural line,

so that they blend in with the walls of the room when painted.

Glass shelves that slot into the two side walls of an alcove look very neat, although achieving this effect is not always possible. Constructing a wooden frame on to which glass shelves can be fitted is a suitable alternative, and also allows you to incorporate wiring for concealed lighting underneath and behind the wooden frame. Glass shelves when lit from above or below look especially attractive.

Sometimes battens or brackets can be used to decorative effect. Specially-made iron brackets can make a very strong feature of shelving in a room.

MADE TO MEASURE

You cannot have the sort of shelving shown on these pages unless they are built specifically for the space into which they fit. Fitted shelves are an important asset in a living room. They provide open storage which is unique to that room and lend an individual character to it. Bought shelves which vaguely fill a space can never complement the shape and dimensions of a room in the same way.

In two of the rooms, whole walls have been shelved to great effect. A large collection of books (opposite) stretches from floor to ceiling and frames an existing window and radiator. A more problematic space has been filled (center) allowing the sloping ceiling to dictate the dimensions of the shelving structure ensuring a strong, architectural quality.

ALCOVE SHELVES

In two modern interiors, alcoves have been specifically created to carry display shelves. These can be easily incorporated into a do-it-yourself scheme using a false wall or building out from an existing wall to form an alcove.

In a large expanse of wall (top) the alcove of shelves breaks up an otherwise flat area and is filled with an informal arrangement of objects. Because of the defined shelf area, the effect remains neat and contained.

A half-wall screens two sections of a room (below) and has been left hollow to carry attractive inset glass shelves.

Tailor-made Display

GLORIOUS GLASS

Glass shelves are particularly effective for displays because they are narrow, unobtrusive, and transparent. They can be supported by various means: simple studs support smoked glass (opposite above left) which beautifully displays a collection of fossils. It is easier to use glass in an alcove such as this, or in a sloping recess (opposite below right) formed above a low closet. The glass is not vulnerable to damage by protruding into the room, so it can safely hold delicate objects such as these antique glasses.

Where a glass shelf is not contained within a framework the supports must be very strong. Metal bars (opposite above right) hold thick glass shelves which are also being secured by the back wall into which they have been recessed for added support.

Tough steel wire (available from ships' chandlers) is partially obscured by a hanging ornament (opposite below center), and runs through holes in the glass to suspend these shelves. Give glass shelves a light source from above so that diffused light filters through to illuminate the objects below.

COLOR FOR CONTRAST

The understatement of glass is one way of enhancing a display. A colorful setting can offer another. In an emerald green room (opposite below left) the vivid wall color has been carried on to the shelves to blend them with the room and to provide a stunning background for books and objects. The thick, hollow shelves conceal their supports to give an architectural unity.

PERCHED ON THE WALL

Individual perches have been created for a collection of decoy ducks and carved birds (left) to form a truly original grouping on one wall. A perfect example of an imaginative display, tailor-made for a special collection.

FIREPLACES AND HEARTHS

Fireplaces should be considered in two ways. The first is as a source of heat. If that source of heat is a wood- or coal-burning fire with all the associated warm glow, comfort and well-being, then your living room has a great natural asset. It may be dirty, wasteful of energy, hard work, and highly impractical, but you can only curl up and feel really cozy in front of a *real* fire. Radiators, under-floor heating, electric and gas fires hardly compensate, though some highly realistic coal-effect gas fires are available.

You may want to re-open an existing fireplace that has been blocked off. Tampering with electricity or gas in any way involves checking local codes concerning utilities. It is often safer, and sometimes essential, to leave the removal of gas or electric heating fixtures to professionals. You must also check that a fireplace is unblocked satisfactorily, that the flue is not cracked or damaged (which could lead to the escape of noxious fumes), and that the grate you install is both suitable and efficient for the situation. Get a professional to check the fireplace before you make any changes yourself.

The second consideration of the fireplace is as a focal point for the room and its decorative scheme. A full-fledged fire surround and mantel form a dominating feature in a room. Removing and replacing a surround is often simpler than you may imagine, but the task is a building, rather than a decorating, one. The work will probably involve some brick and plaster work as well as woodwork. Seek professional guidance and do not undertake the task unless you feel confident in your ability to do the work well. When installing a grate and the surrounding fireproof bricks or metal shield, your work should be checked very carefully, since any work which is less than perfect could lead to serious cracks or even an

FOCAL POINTS

A number of inventive design ideas are combined in an outstanding open fireplace (above). The chimney breast is flanked by windows which give added prominence to the fireplace; a magnificent slab of marble forms the raised hearth. The fireplace is a simple square framed in galvanized steel, perfectly suited to the style of the room. Above the fireplace is a clever variation on the traditional mantel shelf. A small shelf has been built into the chimney breast and a pretty arched alcove curves above it.

A more traditional approach (center) is seen in this wooden fire surround and mantel, designed to match the adjoining dado rail and paneling details. The wood is finished with a subtle paint technique that highlights the decorative detailing, while a warm glow from the flames is reflected from the metal fire backing.

PURE AND SIMPLE

A simple but effective design (below) reduces the fireplace to an opening framed in brick and wood. It can be just as important to remove a decorative fireplace from a room as to add one to it, especially if you want the room to have a modern atmosphere. Again, the wooden frame echoes other adjoining woodwork – here, it is the baseboard. The hearth has also been reduced: it is merely a row of heat-resistant stones that abut with the wooden floor.

outbreak of fire. Never underestimate the disruption and mess to the living room which this whole process will involve.

The style of your fireplace will affect the style of the room. A grand installation will add distinction to a period room, but may look ridiculous in more modest surroundings. As a general rule, try to match the period of the fireplace to that of the room. Removing an ugly recent design in a Victorian building and replacing it with an original Victorian fireplace will undoubtedly improve the room, particularly if your overall scheme involves restoring period architectural details throughout the house.

Alternatively, you may wish to reduce rather than enhance the impact of the fireplace. Taking out an overbearing monstrosity and leaving a neat opening, edged, perhaps, with a rim of galvanized steel or with plain white heat-resistant tiles, will suit a more clean-cut and minimal room. You do not have to replace a mantel if you want a plain surround and it may suit your scheme to do away with the fireplace altogether and present a flat-fronted chimney breast. Another option would be to use the hollow chimney breast for built-in shelving and display.

There is an enormous range of period, reproduction, and modern grates available, as well as fireplace surrounds so it may be interesting to design and build your own fireplace. Your work must be of a high quality since a fireplace is such a focal point in a room. You can use exposed or plastered brickwork, or wood to great effect. Marble slabs for a grate and slips for a surround are also a possibility. You can buy period tiles, reproductions of traditional designs, or contemporary tiles. Whatever approach you decide to take, do not begin until you have a clear design to follow or an example to copy.

A PERFECT SETTING

An old setting serves as a reminder of the original architectural character in an otherwise sweeping redesign of an Arts and Crafts villa (above). The chimney has had its adjoining walls removed to open up the ground floor, and it now acts as an impressive screen between living and dining areas. This delightful iron and tile fireplace with its decorative wood mantel could be an inspiration for a home-built fireplace. Alternatively, a period fireplace can be salvaged, or bought from a specialist and installed in a living room. Take care to choose a fireplace which suits the era and decorative scheme of the room.

Another fireplace which perfectly combines with the style of the room is this one in natural brick (center). In a relaxed living room, the warm, mellow tones of the brick match the furnishings and objects. A brick fireplace is not beyond the building capabilities of a good amateur bricklayer.

MODERN AND MINIMAL

A striking design in a minimal modern room (below). The fireplace surround is made from high quality heat-resistant ceramic tiles which carry over from the floor. The energy source is provided by gas, not a real fire, and allows for the use of these exotic, indestructible, volcanic rocks as "fuel." The grate is formed by a basket of galvanized steel, and a panel of specially heat-resistant glass is used for the reflective backing.

FLOORING

In many houses the living room has a variety of roles to play. It is not just somewhere to sit, relax, and entertain: often it has to double as a playroom, a study, a library, a television room, and maybe even a dining area.

All of these functions have to be taken into account when choosing the flooring. One thing is certain: the room will be in constant use, so the flooring must be capable of withstanding a lot of wear.

Although the flooring will run from wall-to-wall in most cases, it can be combined with other floor coverings. For example, a varnished wooden floor with a central square of carpet or a rug laid on it can be most effective.

If you prefer a hard floor, then tiles – whether ceramic, quarry, marble, slate, or stone – can all be used in living rooms if the setting is right. They can be softened by the addition of rag rugs and dhurries.

Wood, of course, is an excellent flooring material. You can lay a new wood-strip or wood-block surface over an existing floor, or you can use the existing wooden floorboards, as long as they are in good condition.

RESTORING A WOODEN FLOOR

Take a good look at the floor to make sure it is suitable for restoration. If it is very badly worn, it may need to be completely renovated, or covered with an entirely new wooden floor.

If there are wide gaps between the floorboards, fill them with wooden strips. These should be planed along their length to form a slight taper. Apply aliphatic resin adhesive to the sides, and then tap the strips into place in the gaps. Allow the glue to set, then plane the strips level with the surface of the floor.

If the floorboards are uneven because of heavy wear that is no more than about $\frac{1}{8}$in (3mm) deep, it may be possible to resurface the floor by sanding it smooth. If the floorboards have worn more deeply, either replace them, or turn the affected boards upside down and re-lay them. Alternatively, cover the floor with plywood and lay a new wood-strip or block floor over the top.

If your floorboards are old, try to replace the worn ones with matching old boards from a secondhand lumberyard or an architectural salvage yard. New boards, even when they are stained to match the old ones, will tend to stand out.

RE-LAYING FLOORBOARDS

If there are damaged boards, or many wide gaps between boards, it will be best to lift the old boards by prying them up, so that the best boards can be relaid without gaps, and replacement boards fitted to fill the empty spaces.

After removing the old boards, pull out the old fixing nails. Re-lay the boards, ensuring that they are tightly pressed together, by using folding wedges (see **Techniques, page 81**) between each block of four or five boards and a scrap of wood temporarily nailed to the joists. Nail boards in place before removing wedges and laying another four or five boards.

BLEACHED WOOD

This impressive wood floor has been bleached, given a pale paint wash, and then varnished for durability. It will not resist heavy wear but can be easily restored, and provides a beautiful background for the room.

LUXURIOUS MARBLE

Marble slips have a splendid impact on a room and can be used effectively in bathrooms and halls as well as living rooms. Marble is a cold and hard substance; however, it is also undeniably luxurious.

PAINTED WOOD

In a large loft space, a wooden floor has been painted pure white. If you are prepared to retouch it regularly, and use existing boards which are less than perfect, this is a simple solution to a broad expanse of floor.

RESURFACING A FLOOR BY SANDING

Make sure that all floorboards are securely nailed down. Any that are split or badly damaged should be replaced. Pull out protruding carpet tacks, and with a hammer and nailset, drive down the heads of the board-fixing nails so that they are about $\frac{1}{8}$in (3mm) below the surface.

You should rent an industrial floor sander for treating the main part of the floor, with a smaller hand disc sander or belt sander for finishing the edges near the baseboards.

The floor sander looks like a giant vacuum cleaner with a revolving drum around which abrasive sheets are attached. Although floor sanders have dust extraction bags, these are not entirely effective, so wear a dust mask and old clothes. Before starting, open the windows in the room and use masking tape to seal around doors leading to adjacent rooms.

The sander should be used along the length of the floorboards, never across them, as this can cause scratches.

Tilt the sander back before switching on, then gradually lower it to the floor and allow it to move forward under its own power, restraining it slightly so that it does not travel too fast. Work forwards and backwards in a line with the boards, overlapping each pass by 2in (50mm).

After the main area has been sanded, sand the edges with the hand machine. Finish corners with a scraper and a hand sanding block. Finally, vacuum the floor and wipe over it with alcohol.

FINISHING TREATMENTS

Staining Any replacement boards that are lighter in color than the rest should be stained darker. With a rag, apply the stain and rub it evenly into the wood to bring out the desired color. Remember that most clear finishes deepen the color of the wood, so test it first in a corner.

Sealing Floorboards can be sealed with several coats of one- or two-part polyurethane-based varnish/sealer which dries to a clear gloss, satin, or matte finish on the surface. Alternatively, use an oil-based sealer, which will soak into the surface to give a scratch-resistant sheen. To darken the color of the floor, use a varnish stain or simply polish the floor with wax.

Liming This technique involves rubbing a white pigment into the grain of the wood before sealing it. It is easiest to use white paint thinned with turpentine since these materials are readily available, but you can use limed wax or gesso, which is plaster of Paris. Paint the liming mixture along the boards, covering a small area at a time, and wipe the mixture off with rags, leaving a white stain in the cracks. Finally, seal the floor with varnish.

Painting If there are many new floorboards, painting will avoid a patchy appearance. Apply undercoat and two coats of a hard-wearing oil-based gloss paint, or a satin finish paint.

COIR MATTING

The natural quality of coir matting has a similar decorative effect to wood and is often a good alternative. In its own right, it is very popular as a muted, warm background for many styles of room, ancient or modern.

CONTEMPORARY WOOD

Wooden floors are available today in a vast range, and many of them are easily installed by an amateur. They are usually sold in sections. This broad-planked floor in pale wood is especially suitable for a light and airy studio.

PERIOD WOOD

Old wood floors, provided the boards have not been partially replaced and are in a reasonable condition, can be beautifully restored by stripping and finishing. They can be stained or oiled to deepen the tone of the wood.

ROOMS TO WORK IN

If you work at home, installing a personal workspace will be a major priority when it comes to designing your home. Equally, you may need a private den or study, a well-equipped workshop, a sewing room or a darkroom. Whatever your requirements, if you have a limited budget, you will achieve something far more comfortable, efficient, and practical by designing and building it yourself than by installing ready-made fixtures.

Few home improvement tasks are more satisfying than creating a room, or a section of a room, which is a pleasure to work in. Unlike the rest of your home, you will probably not be sharing a work space or using it for tasks other than those for which it is specifically designed, so you are free to indulge yourself and create your ideal personal work space.

By adapting the projects in this book, you will find that you can create precisely what you need for a tailor-made workroom, whether it is a wall-mounted unit of pigeon-hole shelving, a simple desk top made from a door, or a bulletin board.

DOWN TO WORK

The ultimate Modernist environment for a designer – a pure white minimal room (above) – has a work area separated from the main room by the simple, but highly effective, device of a raised back to a desk unit.

An ingenious use of space on one side of a bedroom (opposite) where high storage shelves are reached by a sliding ladder. A drawing board is fitted into a high-level worksurface partly supported by an attractive stack of drawers. The window is left intact.

HOME OFFICE

Whether you work from home, or merely want a private area for paperwork and home management, for your children to study in, or for your own reading and contemplation, then you must first allocate the amount of space that can be given over to your home office.

A small room is ideal, but if this is not possible or practical, there are many ways to screen off a section or corner of a living room or bedroom, part of a hallway or landing, or even a part of the garage. Work areas should be neither too enclosed nor over exposed. A movable screen may be the answer, so that the room or landing can be easily returned to its original dimensions. Build one in wood, create a Japanese version using stretched paper or fabric, or buy an old or ready-made one, budget permitting. Of course, an effective work area can be made without a partition or screen, but you must define the work space or be prepared for it to spread across the room.

Once the area is defined, plan the office with care and work out precisely what you need to build: a desk or writing surface, shelving, pigeon-holes, display boards, and storage. Keep it simple and remember the practical limitations of wire management, lighting, and comfort.

The desktop can be made from an old door, a plain section of wood, or a bought trestle or desk. Position it close to a natural light source and ensure that all shelves and storage areas are within easy reach when you are sitting at the desk.

We live in the age of the computer. Storing paperwork, files, and notes is no longer any more important than wiring-in the electrical equipment, calculators, personal computer, printer, and keyboard. The development of new technology in the business office has spread across to the home office and the study. Children now use computers to help them study as well as to play computer games for entertainment. These activities are as much a part of their lives as reading or playing with toys.

If you want to build a safe, comfortable workstation incorporating a computer system, then consider the following factors: a surface to carry a keyboard should be lower than a writing desk to ensure that your wrists are not bent and straining when typing; lighting should not interfere with the screen, but should focus on to the desk or writing surface. Invest in a really good office chair rather than risk back injury, and make sure that the room is well-ventilated and adequately heated.

OFFICE STORAGE

The sparse and functional office of a fashion designer has simple adjustable shelving on a standard system of brackets (opposite above). On one wall, the shelves are backed with felt to form a bulletin board.

A unit of closets, with some sliding and some hinged doors (below left), provides ample hidden storage for all office clutter behind a modern desk.

A storage unit which doubles as a screen separating a work area (below right) has access to drawers and cupboards on one side and a fitted desk forms the other.

To display her creative work, a sculptor has suspended glass shelves from strong steel wires (opposite below right) in her home workroom. Hidden storage is cleverly provided by shelves obscured by a Venetian blind.

A PLACE FOR A DESK

In an alcove, a desk is simply a laminated board (opposite below center) offset by two beautiful classic folding chairs.

In a small area adjoining a living room (below center) a wooden structure supports a wide worksurface and extends to form a fitted sofa.

A mezzanine floor has been built-in to a house to create a delightful open office area (opposite below left).

MAKING AN ENTRANCE

There is great potential for home improvements in entrances, hallways, passages, and landings. The front door itself and the area immediately outside it should be welcoming and attractive, perhaps providing shelter and certainly making the transition from outside to indoors as comfortable and convenient as possible.

The entrance hall to any building is important. It sets the scene for what is to come and allows an area for hellos and goodbyes. An entrance that leads directly into a room is rarely ideal, so maintain your hallway at all costs, even if it may appear at first to be a waste of precious living space.

Passages, stairways, and landing are not only the spaces between rooms but are also areas that can be utilized for storage and display, work areas or places to sit.

They should be decorated, planned, and restored with as much care and attention as the living room.

In period homes, the architectural details in the hallways and on the stairs are often neglected or allowed to deteriorate, so concentrate on restoring them to their former glory. In modern buildings, make the entrance as atmospheric as possible and ensure that the lighting is subtle but functional. A common problem, especially for entrance halls, is the clutter that naturally accumulates there – everything from muddy boots, umbrellas, and overcoats, to bicycles, strollers, and unwanted furniture. Create a proper storage area for essential items and discard unwanted objects. Do not forget to buy a large doormat: mud, grit, and moisture can quickly ruin a hall carpet.

FLOOR TO CEILING

An open hall has durable, white ceramic tiles (above left) which reflect the natural light. A fitted closet provides storage.

The hall is defined by a large area of fitted matting (above right). Where walls have been removed in a conversion, a curved wall is a useful and attractive form of transition from hall to living area. Downlighters are suitable for halls and passages. Lights which hang or protrude from the ceiling break up a narrow space and are easily knocked if furniture is being moved.

A wall given over to fitted closets in a passage-way (opposite) provides spacious storage in a compact area. Two types of flooring add to the style of this hall and stairway, with slate used in the entrance and blond wood for the stairs and landing.

Below Stairs

An office has utilized an otherwise dead space below stairs (above) in a hallway. Simple shelves on battens form open storage for books and files. A false back hides wire for lamps and for the personal computer, while a broad shelf forms the desk top.

Open Cloakroom

In a corner of a hall (right), an open cloakroom has been created, reminiscent of a locker room. Across an alcove, the stylish but practical grid of poles provides a useful hanging space and a shoe storage area. Great care has been taken in choosing and mixing pale colors and natural textures to open up and lighten the area. Bleached and white-washed wood paneling is used on some walls and on the ceiling, while other walls have exposed brickwork, painted white. The area is given an added sense of space by the large expanse of mirror.

Building and remodeling projects in halls and passage-ways are dependent on several factors: you may want to restore and highlight moldings, paneling, banisters, dado rails, doors, architraves, or the floor in a period hallway. Ugly gas and electricity meters, wires coming from outside the house, and door bells and alarms may benefit from boxing-in.

You can improve the appearance and character of a dark, tunnel-like hall by replacing a solid door that leads from it with a glazed one, or even by installing an interior window to allow light to enter from another room.

Apart from good restoration and deco-ration, the most important way to improve your entrance and passage-ways is to take a long hard look at the lighting. Such areas often have only an overhead pendant light or two, or unflattering fluorescent strips. Consider installing wall-lights or spotlights on dimmer switches so that a low level of light can be maintained through the night for security reasons. Taking into account the fact that furniture will be moved through the passages and could damage protruding or hanging fixtures, downlighters can be very practical. Decide on your lighting solutions before you undertake restoration or decoration so that you can orga-

TRADITIONAL DISPLAY

The color, style, and impact of a beautifully crafted display unit in a hallway (left) perfectly suits the decorative old tin cans it holds and the architecture of the house. The design, which has been carried up beside the stairs, uses tongue-and-groove paneling and architraves to form separate compartments for the display. In eighteenth- and nineteenth-century houses, pine was painted over, using deep colors rather than left in its natural state.

A HALL OF BOOKS

Beneath the stairs in an ample hallway is the perfect place for extra bookshelves provided they are created to fit precisely the wall they are placed on (above).

nize the wiring and fixtures without disrupting the pristine cleanliness of newly decorated surfaces.

If space is limited elsewhere in your home, take a look around your hall, passage-ways, and landings to see how you can free up extra space for storage and display. All sorts of dead space, empty walls, and under-utilized corners are to be found there. If you follow the guidelines on structural shelving and fitted storage in this book, then rows of book shelves or fitted closets can be built in passages without destroying the dimensions. Designers often integrate floor-to-ceiling closets into halls, with flush doors to give the appearance of a blank wall, behind which all manner of clutter can be conveniently tidied away.

Neat coat hooks can be made into a feature in an entrance hall and a shoe rack can be an attractive addition. Somewhere to place mail, newspapers, circulars, and the many other small items that can congregate near the front door, is also an advantage. A hall table may be the solution but you could consider a unit combining shelves, hooks, and a shoe rack.

If you are desperately in need of a home office space or work area, then do not rule out a corner of the hall or the area under the stairs as a possible solution.

ALCOVE SHELVES AND CUPBOARDS

Many rooms have a chimney breast with an alcove on either side. This design allows you to integrate storage space into an alcove without disturbing the unity of the wall. This is achieved by repeating a triangular molding from the face of the alcove cupboard doors on a decorative panel over the fireplace. Larger moldings of the same shape also form the wall supports for the alcove shelves in the recesses, and for the angled valance which conceals the incandescent strip lights. The repetition of this decorative device provides a unifying element to the design and detailing of the whole wall.

How you decorate the shelves, doors, and panels is dependent on your scheme for the rest of the room. This project is an example of my philosophy that tries to ensure that fixtures which are built-in to the structure of a room blend into the existing architecture and features rather than argue with them.

SECTION OF
CUPBOARD DOOR

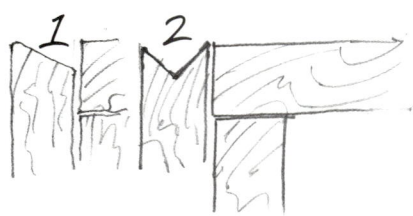

top edge of doors
can be beveled
in two ways to
provide a firm
grip

PLAN OF CUPBOARD
& WALL DECORATION

triangular battens
glued & nailed
to door panels —
then filled &
painted.

FRONT ELEVATION.

Triangular shelf-support battens echo the shape of the door & wall decoration

Wall decoration echoes door panels

Concealed lighting at back of shelves.

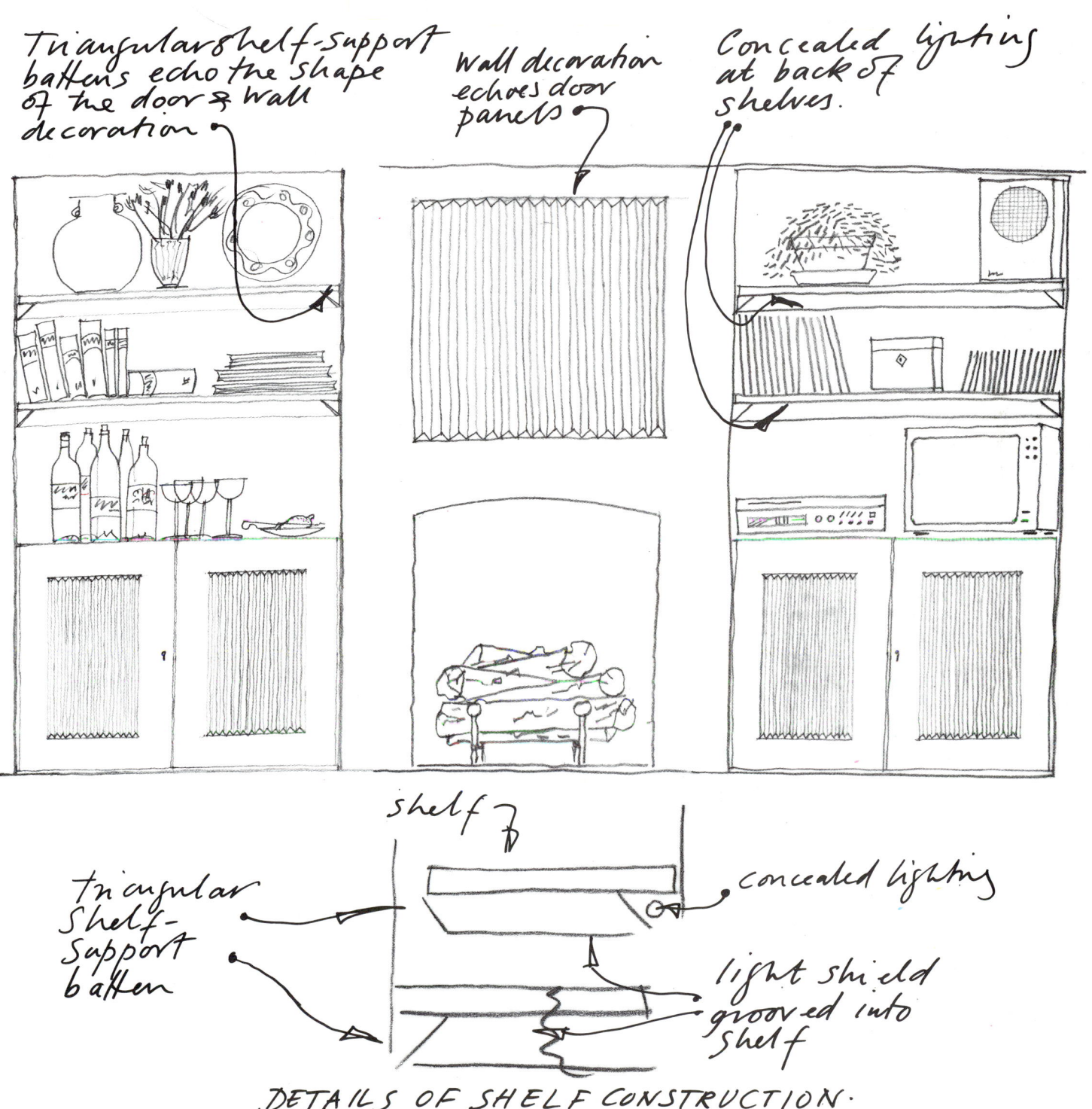

triangular shelf-support batten

shelf

concealed lighting

light shield grooved into shelf

DETAILS OF SHELF CONSTRUCTION.

ALCOVE SHELVES AND CUPBOARDS

Living rooms always call for a reasonable amount of storage and display space; one way of creating it is to make use of the wasted space on each side of a chimney breast, or in a corner, by installing shelves and a cupboard. A basic design is described below, but the project is easy to adapt to suit your own requirements. You may want alcove shelves and cupboards to house a television, stereo equipment, books, drinks and glasses, or favorite ob-

jects. The function will probably determine the height of your cupboards and shelves, so think about your specific storage needs before you start work. For example, you may want to construct just one cupboard for use as a mini-bar. Alternatively, you may like to vary the number of shelves above a cupboard according to the size, type, and combination of objects you wish to store or display on them.

The "linenfold" decoration which

has been added to the cupboard doors here is echoed on the wall with a panel of the same design, adding an individual and interesting detail. By varying the kind of molding you use on the cupboards and on the wall, you will be able to adapt the overall design to suit your own decorative scheme. Another way of adding a personal touch to the finished project is to vary the cupboard door hardware by using different door handles or knobs.

Whatever the design, it is most important to ensure that all gaps are filled and edges are smoothed so that the cupboards and shelves appear to be part of the structure of the room, even if they are not painted the same color. The shelf battens should be disguised as much as possible to blend in with the wall. In this project, we show how a shelf batten can incorporate a light above a shelf, lending muted tones to the color scheme of the walls.

TOOLS

STEEL BENCH RULE

UTILITY KNIFE

TRY SQUARE

SCRIBING BLOCK

CARPENTER'S LEVEL

HAND SAW (or circular saw)

BACK SAW

CHISEL (bench type)

DRILL (hand or power)

DRILL BITS

MASONRY DRILL BIT

COUNTERSINK BIT

FORSTNER BIT for fitting concealed hinges

POWER SABER SAW

SANDING BLOCK and SANDING PAPER (or finishing sander)

HAND PLANE (or power plane)

HAMMER

MALLET

NAILSET

MATERIALS For one alcove

Part	Quantity	Material	Length*
UPRIGHTS	2	2 × 2in (50 × 50mm) S4S softwood	As required (ours are 34in [865mm])
HORIZONTAL RAILS	2	2 × 2in (50 × 50mm) S4S softwood	Width of alcove, less 4in (100mm)
BACK SUPPORT BATTENS	2	1 × 2in (25 × 50mm) S4S softwood	Width of alcove
SIDE SUPPORT BATTENS	4	1 × 2in (25 × 50mm) S4S softwood	Depth of alcove, less 4in (100mm)
BASE FRONT- AND BACK- SUPPORT BATTENS	2	1 × 1in (25 × 25mm) S4S softwood	Width of alcove
BASE SIDE-SUPPORT BATTENS	2	1 × 1in (25 × 25mm) S4S softwood	Depth of alcove
ALCOVE SHELF-SUPPORT BACK BATTENS	2	1½in (38mm) triangular section	Width of alcove
ALCOVE SHELF-SUPPORT SIDE BATTENS	4	1½in (38mm) triangular section	Depth of alcove, less 1½in (38mm)
"LINENFOLD" WALL PANEL DECORATION	As required	1½in (38mm) triangular section	Height of wall panel
"LINENFOLD" DOOR DECORATION	12 per door	1in (25mm) triangular section	Door height, less 8in (200mm)
DOWELS	1	Approximately 6ft (1.8m) hardwood doweling	As required
BASE PANEL	1	⅛in or ¼in (4mm or 6mm) plywood	Alcove width × depth, less thickness of baseboard and front frame
CUPBOARD SHELF	1	¾in (19mm) MDF, lumber core, or particleboard	Alcove width × depth of alcove, less 3in (75mm)
TOP PANEL	1	As above	Alcove width × depth
DOORS	2	¾in (19mm) MDF	½ alcove width, less ⅜in (8mm) × front frame height less 1in (25mm)
ALCOVE SHELVES	2	1in (25mm) MDF	Alcove width × alcove depth, less 1in (25mm)
CENTER WALL PANEL	1	¼in (6mm) MDF or plywood	As required

*Approximate lengths only – refer to copy for actual size.

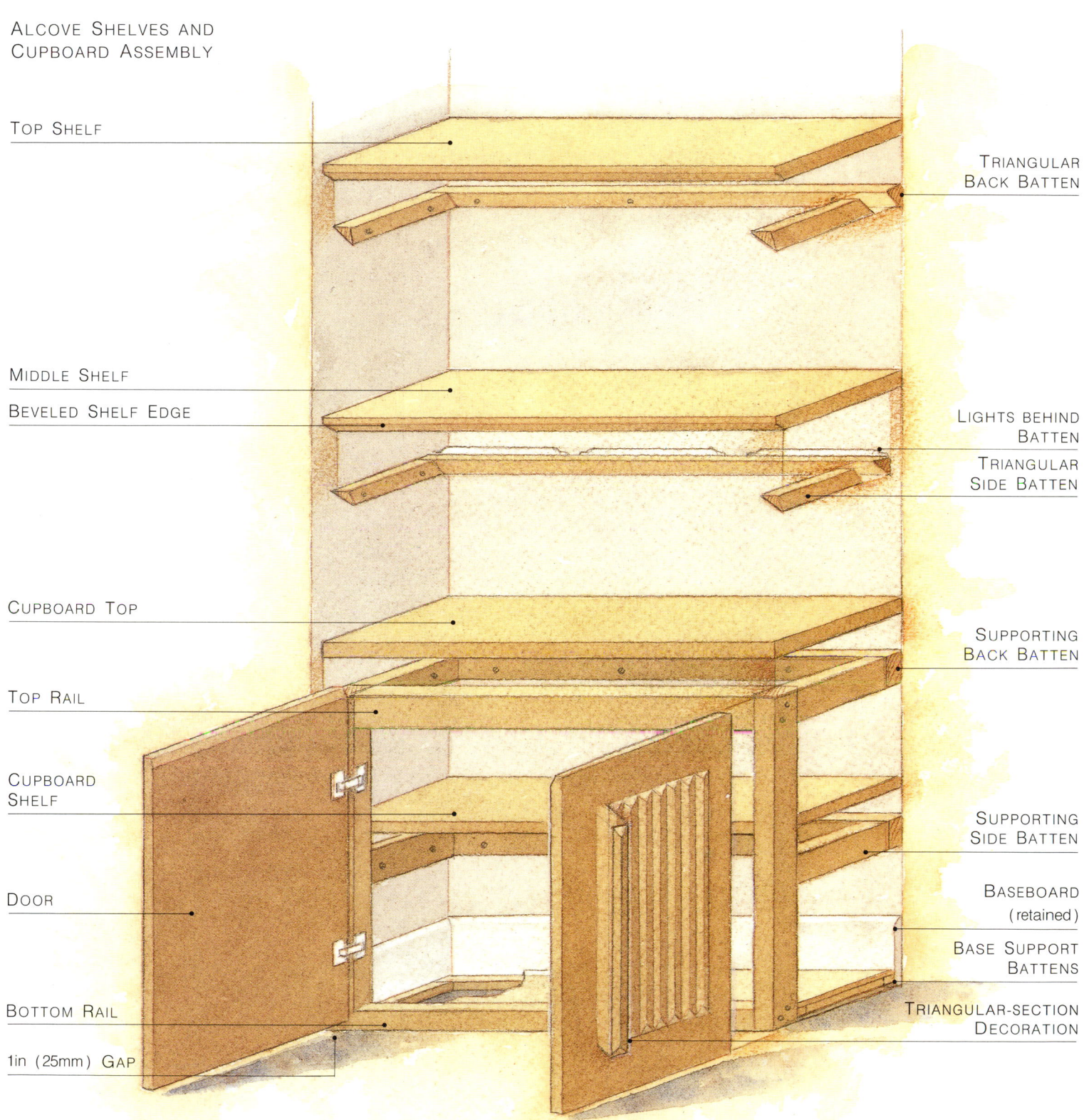

ALCOVE SHELVES AND
CUPBOARD ASSEMBLY

TOP SHELF

TRIANGULAR
BACK BATTEN

MIDDLE SHELF

BEVELED SHELF EDGE

LIGHTS BEHIND
BATTEN

TRIANGULAR
SIDE BATTEN

CUPBOARD TOP

SUPPORTING
BACK BATTEN

TOP RAIL

CUPBOARD
SHELF

SUPPORTING
SIDE BATTEN

DOOR

BASEBOARD
(retained)

BASE SUPPORT
BATTENS

BOTTOM RAIL

TRIANGULAR-SECTION
DECORATION

1in (25mm) GAP

THE CUPBOARDS

MAKING THE FRAME

Using 2 × 2in (50 × 50mm) S4S (smooth 4 sides) lumber, cut two uprights to the desired height, allowing for the thickness of the top. The height of our cupboards, including the top, is 34in (865mm).

Measure for two horizontal rails so that they fit inside the uprights, and cut these from the same size of lumber as used for the uprights. Before jointing the frame it must be held square with a bracing batten (*see* **Techniques, page 80**). Glue the horizontal rails between the uprights, holding the frame square with bar clamps. When the glue has set, drill into the ends of the horizontal rails through the side rails and insert two lengths of $\frac{1}{2}$in (12mm) dowel into each joint (*see* **Techniques, Dowel joints, page 90**).

INSTALLING THE FRAME

To fit the frame into the alcove it will be necessary to scribe the uprights to the wall (*see* **Techniques, page 91**). If there is baseboard around the walls of the alcove, the side rails should be scribed around it. Alternatively, remove small sections of baseboard, using a back saw and a chisel, where the side rails will fit. Another option is to remove the baseboard entirely, although this rarely looks satisfactory.

Set the frame about 1in (25mm) back into the alcove, attaching it in place with two screws and anchors on each side (*see* **Techniques, page 84**). Countersink the screwheads so that the holes can be filled and painted over.

ATTACHING THE SUPPORTING BATTENS

The supporting battens for the cupboard top and for the cupboard shelf are made from 1 × 2in (25 × 50mm) S4S lumber.

Using a carpenter's level, mark a line all the way around the alcove from the top of the frame. Cut the back batten to the full width of the alcove and attach it to the wall, under the line at the back, using screws and anchors to secure it.

Cut two side battens to fit between the back batten and the front frame.

Attach the battens to the wall at the marked lines as before.

Decide on the height of the cupboard shelf or shelves, and cut and fit the supporting battens at the appropriate height, making sure that they are level.

INSTALLING THE BASE

The cupboard base panel is made from $\frac{1}{8}$in (4mm) or $\frac{1}{4}$in (6mm) plywood and is supported at the edges on 1 × 1in (25 × 25mm) battens.

At the front, glue and nail a supporting batten to the inner face of the bottom rail of the front frame. Attach it $\frac{1}{8}$in (4mm) or $\frac{1}{4}$in (6mm) down from the top (depending on the thickness of plywood you are using) so that the base panel will sit flush with the frame.

At the back, glue and nail a similar batten to the baseboard. Use a carpenter's level resting on the bottom rail of the front frame to mark the height of the base panel at the back, and measure down $\frac{1}{8}$in (4mm) or $\frac{1}{4}$in (6mm) to mark the height of the rear base supporting batten so it can be fitted accurately.

Using lumber of the same size, cut side supporting battens to fit between the front and rear battens, and glue and nail these battens to the baseboard at each side.

Cut the plywood base to size, and use brads to attach it to the supporting battens at the front, back, and sides of the frame. Use a plastic filler to fill the join between the base and the frame, and sand it smooth when dry.

INSTALLING THE TOP

Measure the width of the alcove and the depth from the back wall to the front edge of the frame. If the wall is very uneven, increase these measurements to allow the top to be scribed to the wall.

Cut out the top from 1in (25mm) medium-density fiberboard (MDF), lumber core or particleboard. If using lumber core or particleboard, it will need to have a molded front edge for protection and neatness.

Scribe and fit the top in place and attach at the front by screwing up through the frame. At the back, screw down through the top, and do

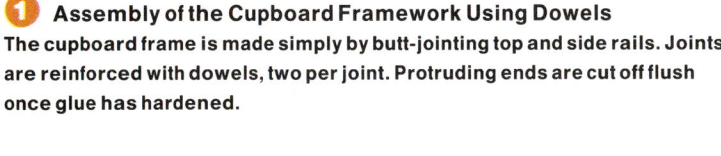

1 **Assembly of the Cupboard Framework Using Dowels**
The cupboard frame is made simply by butt-jointing top and side rails. Joints are reinforced with dowels, two per joint. Protruding ends are cut off flush once glue has hardened.

2 **Installing Cupboard Base**
Battens are placed at front, rear, and sides (not shown). The base is nailed to the top.

3 **Installing the Top Section**
The frame is set back 1in (25mm) from front of alcove. Screw up into top panel.

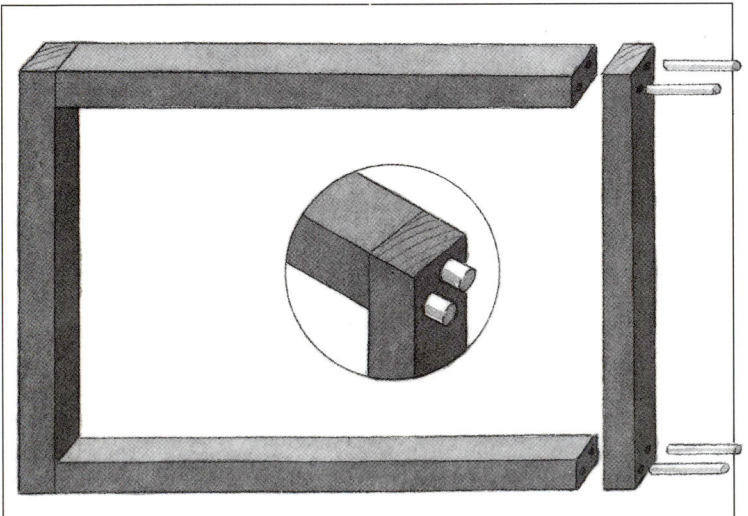

the same at each corner, countersinking the screwheads so that the holes can be filled and painted over neatly when you have finished.

If you are using MDF, plane and sand the front edge flush with the frame. Fill and sand this joint flush.

INSTALLING THE CUPBOARD SHELF

Cut the cupboard shelf from $\frac{3}{4}$in (19mm) MDF, lumber core, or particleboard (with a molded front edge). Make sure it fits, and rest it on supporting battens.

MAKING AND INSTALLING THE DOORS

Using $\frac{3}{4}$in (19mm) MDF, cut two panels to fit the front, flush with the top, but leaving a 1in (25mm) gap at the bottom. The size of the gap at the sides of the doors is determined by the hinges used – consult the manufacturer's instructions. We have used concealed self-closing hinges, and the doors overhang the inner edges of the frame by an amount specified in the manufacturer's instructions (usually about $\frac{5}{8}$in

[15mm]) so that the hinges will operate correctly (*see* **Techniques, page 92**).

To create a finger-grip, bevel the top edge of each door panel to 45° through two-thirds of its thickness, leaving about $\frac{3}{16}$in (5mm) flat on top.

The "linenfold" front detail is created with 1in (25mm) triangular-section birch or pine (fig 4). Measure and mark a square on each door for the "linenfold", leaving a suitable border around the edge (ours is 4in [100mm] at top and bottom, and about $3\frac{1}{2}$in [90mm] at each side). Cut sections to length and bevel the ends to 45° (fig 4).

Mark a center line vertically down the door, and, working outwards from this, glue each length on to the surface, nailing through the side faces in about three places. Continue in each direction until the required number of triangular-shaped sections are attached, with an equal border at each side.

Install the doors using the concealed hinges according to the manufacturer's instructions (*see* **Techniques, page 92**).

●4 Making and Decorating Cupboard Doors
Left Top edges of doors are beveled to provide a fingergrip. **Inset** Attaching "linenfold." **Center** First "linenfold" attached. **Right** Cut a triangular section and bevel the ends to 45°.

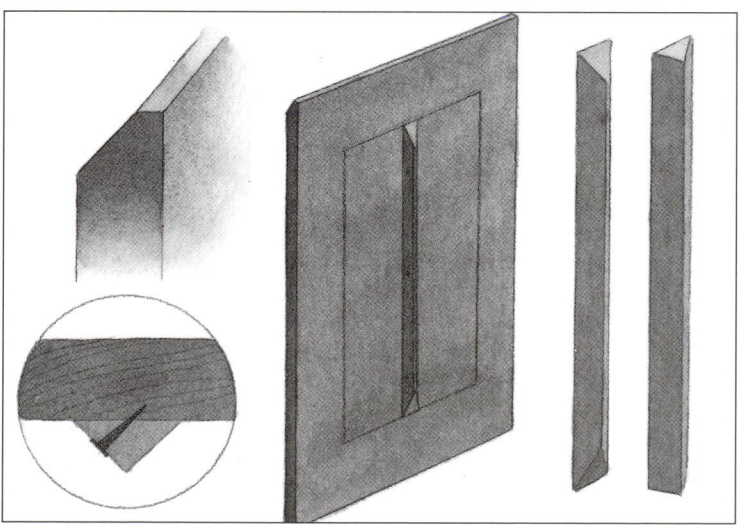

DETAIL OF "LINENFOLD" DOORS
This photograph shows the full effect of the "linenfold" door decoration, together with the neatly beveled fingergrip. You can vary the kind of decoration you use on the door front according to personal taste.

ALCOVE SHELVES AND CUPBOARDS

THE SHELVES

The shelves are made from 1in (25mm) MDF boards supported by 1½in (38mm) triangular battens which are secured to the back and side walls of the alcove.

CUTTING THE TRIANGULAR BATTENS

If you cannot find suitable triangular lumber moldings at your local lumberyard, you can cut them yourself from 2 × 2in (50 × 50mm) S4S lumber using a circular saw.

Tilt your circular saw blade to 45° and cut the lumber diagonally along its length so that it is split into two equal triangular sections. If your saw blade is not large enough to cut right through in one pass, cut partway through and complete the cut with a hand saw. Finally, clean up the sawn faces with a smoothing plane for a neat finish.

If you do not have a suitable circular saw, your lumberyard should easily be able to make this cut for you.

1 **Cutting the Triangular Battens Yourself**
Tilt your circular saw blade to 45° and cut down length of lumber to split it.

INSTALLING THE TOP SHELF

Decide on the height of the top shelf. From the triangular battening, cut a back batten to span the width of the alcove and secure it to the wall.

Cut the side battens to length, which should be the distance from the back of the alcove to 1½in (38mm) in from the front edge. Use triangular battens, and cut a 45° bevel on the front end so that the batten will tail away from the front edge of the shelf. Bevel the back end of the batten in the same direction so that it fits snugly into the corner against the back batten. Attach the side battens in place.

Cut out the shelf from 1in (25mm) MDF to the width of the alcove and to a depth whereby it is set back into the alcove by 1in (25mm). Bevel the front edge of the shelf through the bottom half of its thickness to allow the front edge of the beveled side batten to run flush into the bevel and create an unobtrusive support for the shelf. Screw shelf down into battens. Fill all joints and gaps, and when the filler is hard, sand smooth.

2 **Installing the Shelves**
Top and middle shelves secure on to triangular battens that are screwed to the walls. One batten hides a light.

THE SHELVES IN PLACE
The shelves (above) are 1in (25mm) thick MDF boards which are screwed down to the battens.

SHELVES AND BATTENS
The beveled support battens blend neatly with the beveled front alcove shelves (below).

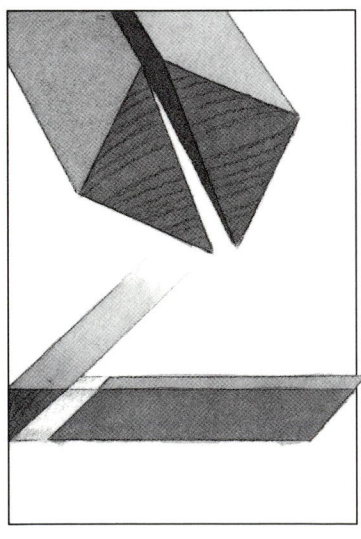

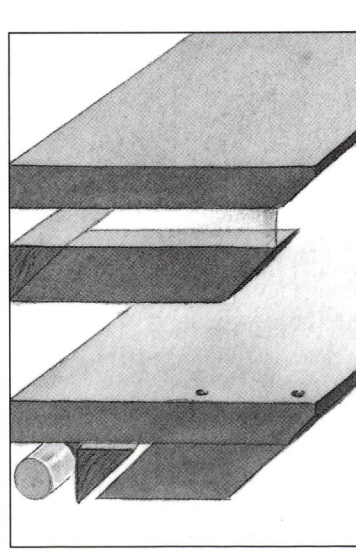

INSTALLING MIDDLE SHELF

Decide on the height of the shelf and cut the back batten to fit into the alcove. In this case the back batten is secured about 3in (75mm) out from the wall so that a light can be installed behind it. Do not attach the batten securely at this stage.

Cut the side battens so that when beveled at front and rear they will be 3in (75mm) away from the wall at the back, and $1\frac{1}{2}$in (38mm) in from the front. Attach the side battens in place, screwing and anchoring them tightly to the alcove wall so that they are both level.

Cut the shelf to size from 1in (25mm) MDF and place it on the side battens, beveling the front as before. Screw it down on to the side battens, countersinking and filling the screwheads.

The back batten, which is cut square at the ends, is positioned under the shelf behind the ends of the side battens. It is secured by screwing down through the shelf. This provides a cover for the light fixtures and also acts as a beam to support the shelf and prevent it from sagging. Countersink the screw holes and fill after inserting the screws. Sand smooth when dry.

LIGHTING

For the concealed lighting under the middle shelf we used three 12in (300mm) long tungsten tube lamps secured behind the back batten.

THE CENTER WALL PANEL

Although not essential to the project, we fitted a center panel on the chimney breast to give a unified look by continuing the theme of the door decoration. The panel is $\frac{1}{4}$in (6mm) MDF or plywood on which $1\frac{1}{2}$in (38mm) triangular-section lumber is glued and nailed. The panel is screwed into the chimney-breast wall using masonry anchors, filled, smoothed, and painted to match the general decoration.

SOFT LIGHTING IN ALCOVES

When lighting is needed, built-in incandescent strips (above) offer a good alternative to the more commonly used fluorescent version.

CONCEALED LIGHTING

The concealed lighting under the middle shelf throws a muted shadow into the alcove and creates a softer atmosphere in the room. Taken from below, this photograph (left) shows the position of the concealed incandescent strip lighting. When viewed from straight on, the lighting is hidden behind the back shelf batten.

RADIATOR COVER

Radiators are often an eye-sore, particularly modern ones. This design offers a solution that screens a radiator from view but still allows a free passage of air and heat; it will look good in a modern or a traditional interior in any room in the house. The design is adaptable for any size

of radiator. The front panel, which lifts off easily for maintenance or adjustment, can be made from vertical or horizontal wooden slats. The wooden cover may be left as natural wood or finished in any color or texture to fit in with your chosen decorative scheme.

If the radiator is a low one, then an excellent alternative design is to make the frame deep enough so that a cushion can be added on top, thereby transforming the radiator cover into a seat. This is particularly effective if your radiator is below a bay window.

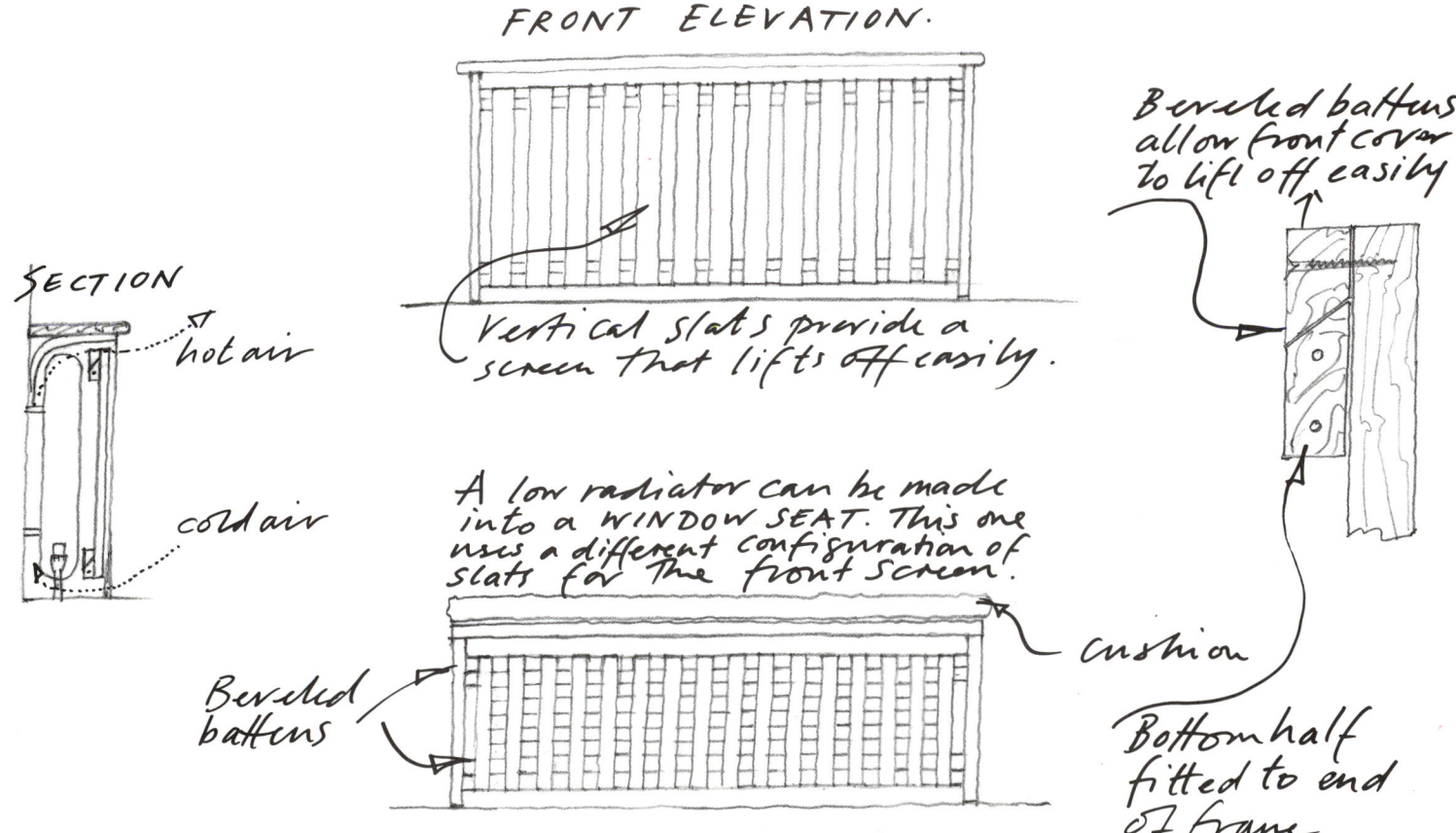

FRONT ELEVATION.

SECTION

hot air

cold air

Vertical slats provide a screen that lifts off easily.

Beveled battens allow front cover to lift off easily

A low radiator can be made into a WINDOW SEAT. This one uses a different configuration of slats for the front screen.

Beveled battens

cushion

Bottom half fitted to end of frame

RADIATOR COVER

The radiator cover can be adapted in size to suit any shape of radiator. With low radiators in an alcove or bay, the shelf and sides can be widened to form an attractive seat. In all cases the front panel is easily removable for decorating, bleeding air from the radiator, or adjusting the valves. Heat-reflecting foil should be attached to the wall behind the radiator with double-sided adhesive tabs. The advantage of a radiator cover is that it can hide an ugly feature of a room. Think about small children when building this project; if there are children in the home, make sure that the front panel of the radiator does not contain gaps that are wide enough for small arms and legs to get caught in.

MAKING THE FRAMEWORK

To calculate the overall dimensions of the cover, measure the length of the radiator to just beyond the valves and measure the height, allowing an extra 2in (50mm) clearance between the top of the radiator and the shelf. Mark these positions on the wall with a pencil.

TOOLS

STEEL MEASURING TAPE

CARPENTER'S LEVEL

HEAT-RESISTANT ADHESIVE

CONTOUR GAUGE

SMALL HAND SAW

CIRCULAR SAW

POWER DRILL (and suitable drill bits)

SABER SAW

SANDING BLOCK and SANDING PAPER

SURFORM

SCREWDRIVERS

MATERIALS

Part	Quantity	Material	Length
SHELF	1	1in (25mm) particleboard or MDF	As required
SIDES	2	1in (25mm) particleboard or MDF	As required
BACK HORIZONTAL BATTEN	1	1 × 3in (25 × 75mm) S4S lumber	Distance between vertical battens
BACK VERTICAL BATTENS	2	1 × 1in (25 × 25mm) S4S lumber	Height of sides
BEVELED BATTENS	4	1 × 4in (25 × 100mm) S4S lumber	Distance between side panels
SLATS	As required	1 × 3in (25 × 75mm) S4S lumber	As required
DOWELS	4	$\frac{1}{4}$in (6mm) dowel	$1\frac{1}{4}$in (30mm)

The side panels should be cut so that they protrude 2–3in (50–75mm) in front of the radiator. The top should overhang the sides by about 2in (50mm) at both ends and protrude 1in (25mm) at the front. Use 1in (25mm) particleboard or

MDF (medium-density fiberboard) for the sides and the top.

ATTACHING THE SIDES

Cut two 1 × 1in (25 × 25mm) lumber battens to the same height as the sides. If there is a baseboard, the

sides of the radiator can be scribed to fit neatly over the baseboard, so that they blend in well with the walls (see **Techniques, page 91**). Similarly, make sure that the battens are cut so that they stop above the baseboard for a neat finish.

1 Marking Top Shelf Batten
Batten is centralized on underside edge of shelf panel, and fixing screw depth is marked.

2 Counterboring Screw Hole
Mark drill bit with tape to depth required and drill holes larger than screwhead.

3 Attaching Sides and Top
Side panels are screwed and anchored to walls. Top shelf attaches to sides on dowels.

4 The Beveled Battens
Using 1 × 4in (25 × 100mm) lumber cut to internal width, saw lengthways at 45° in ratio of $\frac{2}{3}$ to $\frac{1}{3}$.

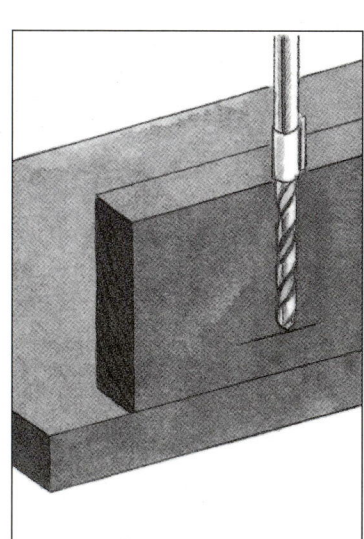

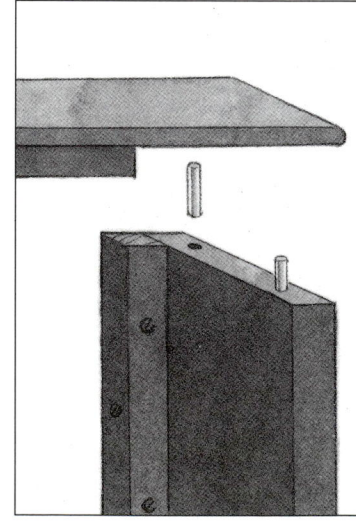

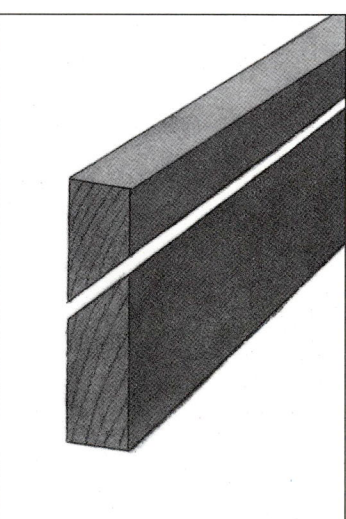

Sawing 81	**Beveled battens 85**
Drilling 83	**Dowel joint 90**
Screwing 84	**Scribing long lengths 91**

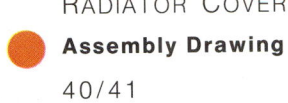

BASIC ASSEMBLY

DOWELS
VERTICAL BATTEN
SIDE PANEL
HIGHER BEVELED BATTEN
HIGHER BEVELED BATTEN
SLATS
TOP SHELF
TOP SHELF BATTEN
VERTICAL BATTEN
LOWER BEVELED BATTEN
SIDE PANEL
LOWER BEVELED BATTEN
FRONT PANEL

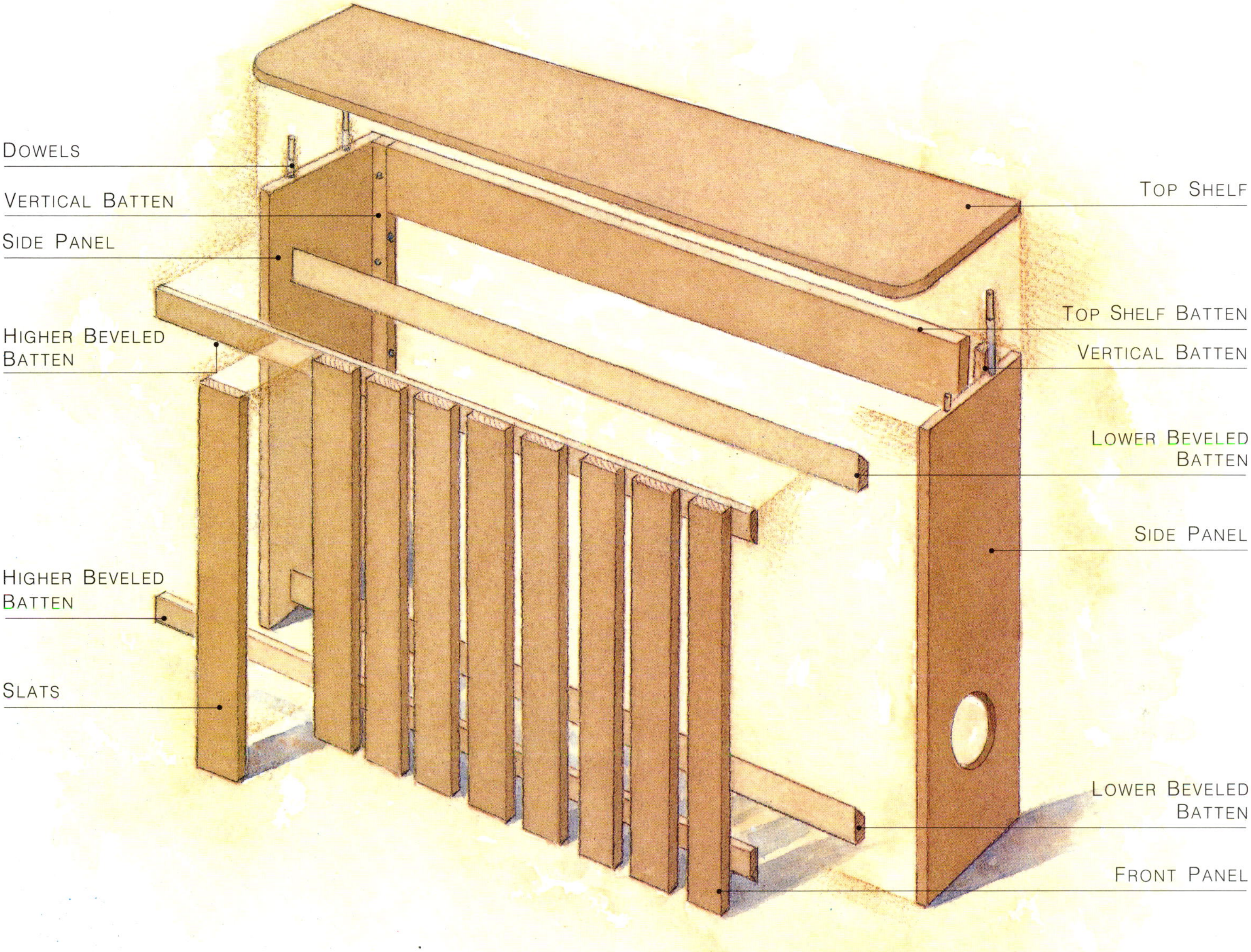

RADIATOR COVER

Drill and countersink the battens on two adjacent faces. Glue and screw them to the inside faces of the sides, flush with the back edges.

For easier access when adjusting the radiator valve, cut a 5in (125mm) diameter hole at a required place in the appropriate side. Drill a hole in a pre-marked circle, then cut around it with a Saber saw. Smooth the edges with sandpaper.

Attach the sides to the wall by screwing through the battens. Check that the sides are plumb.

MAKING THE TOP SHELF

To round off the corners, use a suitable object – a saucer, for example – to mark arcs on them. Cut away the waste with a Saber saw or a coping saw. Round the edges by sanding by hand. This is best done by holding a sheet of sandpaper over the edge with both hands and pulling both sides alternately. Use a sanding block on the corners.

Alternatively, use a router with a $\frac{1}{2}$in (12mm) rounding-over cutter attached to cut the top of the edge and then the bottom of it. Smooth by

sanding down with a block and sandpaper. You may prefer to leave the corners square and to glue a $\frac{1}{2}$in (12mm) half-round molding to the front of the shelf. Tape the molding in place until the glue has set.

Cut a 1 × 3in (25 × 75mm) horizontal batten to fit between the vertical side battens. Lay the shelf upside down on the bench and place the horizontal batten on it so that its ends are equidistant from the ends of the top.

Position a screw by the side of the batten and the back edge of the top shelf, holding it so that the tip is about $\frac{1}{4}$in (6mm) short of the top surface of the shelf. This is to ensure that the screw will not break through to the shelf's surface. Mark off the position of the screwhead on the batten (fig 1, page 40).

Find a drill bit slightly larger than the screwhead. Hold this against the batten with its tip against the position of the screwhead. Fix a piece of tape around the drill bit to indicate the depth to which you should drill. Drill downwards until the tape is at the top edge of the batten (fig 2,

page 40). Glue and screw the batten in place using three equally spaced screws.

THE TOP SHELF

The shelf is doweled to the sides using $\frac{1}{4}$in (6mm) dowels, $1\frac{1}{4}$in (30mm) long (fig 3, page 40). Drill two $\frac{1}{4}$in (6mm) diameter holes in each top edge of the sides. The hole depths should be half the length of the dowels. Transfer the hole positions exactly to the underside of the shelf and again drill $\frac{1}{4}$in (6mm) holes to half the dowel length.

Glue the dowels and the top edges of the sides and place the shelf in position.

THE FRONT PANEL

Measure the length between the sides. Calculate how many 1 × 3in (25 × 75mm) equally spaced vertical slats are required. The width of the spacing is optional, but it is very important that the spaces are not wide enough for a child to get his or her hands, feet, or head accidentally stuck between the slats of the radiator cover front panel.

Measure for the height of the slats, allowing for a 2in (50mm) gap at both top and bottom. Cut the slats to this dimension.

Battens should be cut to the width between the side panels. Cut two from 1 × 4in (25 × 100mm) lumber. To bevel them, use a circular saw set to 45°, cutting lengthwise through each batten to divide it into two portions, one twice the size of the other (fig 4, page 40). The wider portions will be attached between the sides of the cover. The narrower portions will be attached to the slats.

FRONT PANEL ASSEMBLY

Lay out the slats on the bench using a spacing batten between them (*see* **Techniques, page 80**). Lay the pairs of beveled battens in place across the slats so that they are flush with the top and bottom. Make sure that the battens are the right way around – that is, the narrower one is at the top in each case – and lying at the correct angle (fig 1).

Remove the wider battens. Mark the top edge of the bevel on to the back face of the batten, so that you do not screw over this line (fig 2).

Screw the battens to the first slat, using two screws at each end. Continue to screw down the remaining slats using the spacing batten for accurate distribution.

Mark the wider battens where they are to be screwed to the side panels. Either measure down from the top of the side panels or lift up the gate to its correct position.

Drill clearance holes through the sides, then countersink and screw the battens in place.

1 **Assembling Slats and Beveled Battens of Front Panel**
Use a spacing batten to place the slats an equal distance apart with the same space at each end. The battens line up neatly with top and bottom edges of the front panel slats.

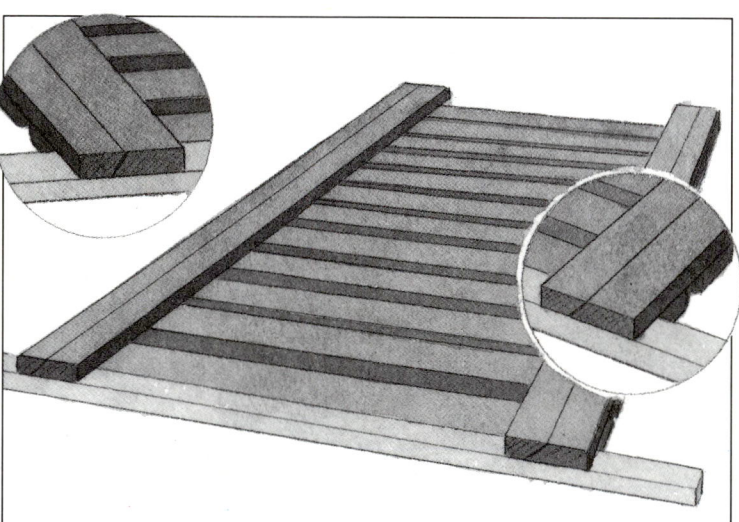

2 **Attaching the Slats**
Scew top (narrow) batten to each slat using two screws. Line on back of slat is screw guide.

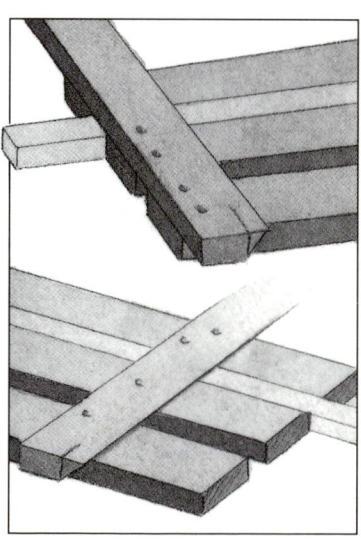

BLENDING A RADIATOR COVER WITH ITS SURROUNDINGS

Cool, luxurious stone has been used wall-to-wall in this Mediterranean-style setting (left) to box-in and cleverly disguise a radiator cover. The result is a stylish, low-level storage or seating area which enhances the painting on the wall above it.

INCORPORATING A RADIATOR IN A DIVIDING WALL

Here two radiators have been built-in to a wall of windows (below left) which divides a porch and a hall. Building-in a radiator cover in this way complements the clean lines of the walls.

SMALL-SPACE LIVING

Many radiators are situated under windows (below center). Here, where space is limited, a shelf has been added above the radiator cover for an extra storage and display area. The cover slats echo the design of the wooden platforms that support the sofa beds.

HIGH CEILING AND TALL WINDOWS

This light and spacious living room (below right) contains two radiator covers which, with the addition of cushions, are adapted to form comfortable window seats.

WALL OF DISPLAY SHELVING

The simplicity, style, and sheer practicality of a wall of shelves with no visible means of support is what I set out to achieve with this design.

I realized that if steel brackets were inserted into the wall and secured, I could then construct hollow-core shelves to slide over the brackets and hide them.

A great advantage of this construction method is that all of the wiring for audio-visual equipment, telephones, and lighting can be contained in the cavity of the shelf rather than trailing around on the surface in an untidy, spaghetti-like mess.

They also give the room a horizontal emphasis as there are no uprights dividing the shelves, which are necessary with conventional shelving to stop the shelves sagging in their lengths.

To complete the shelves I painted them the same color as the wall so that they had a sculptural quality and became part of the fabric of the room.

METAL SUPPORTS

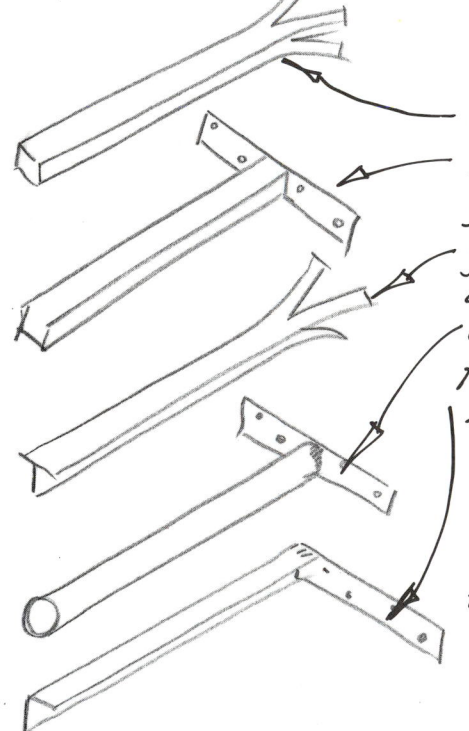

Various metal supports for shelves either grouted into a brick wall or screwed to the surface

when you secure the metal supports to the wall, ensure that they are perfectly aligned to fit the shelf by tying them firmly to a pre-notched length of lumber.

LONGITUDINAL SECTION

metal support inserted into shelf frame

plywood skin

ALIGN YOUR SUPPORTS

metal support

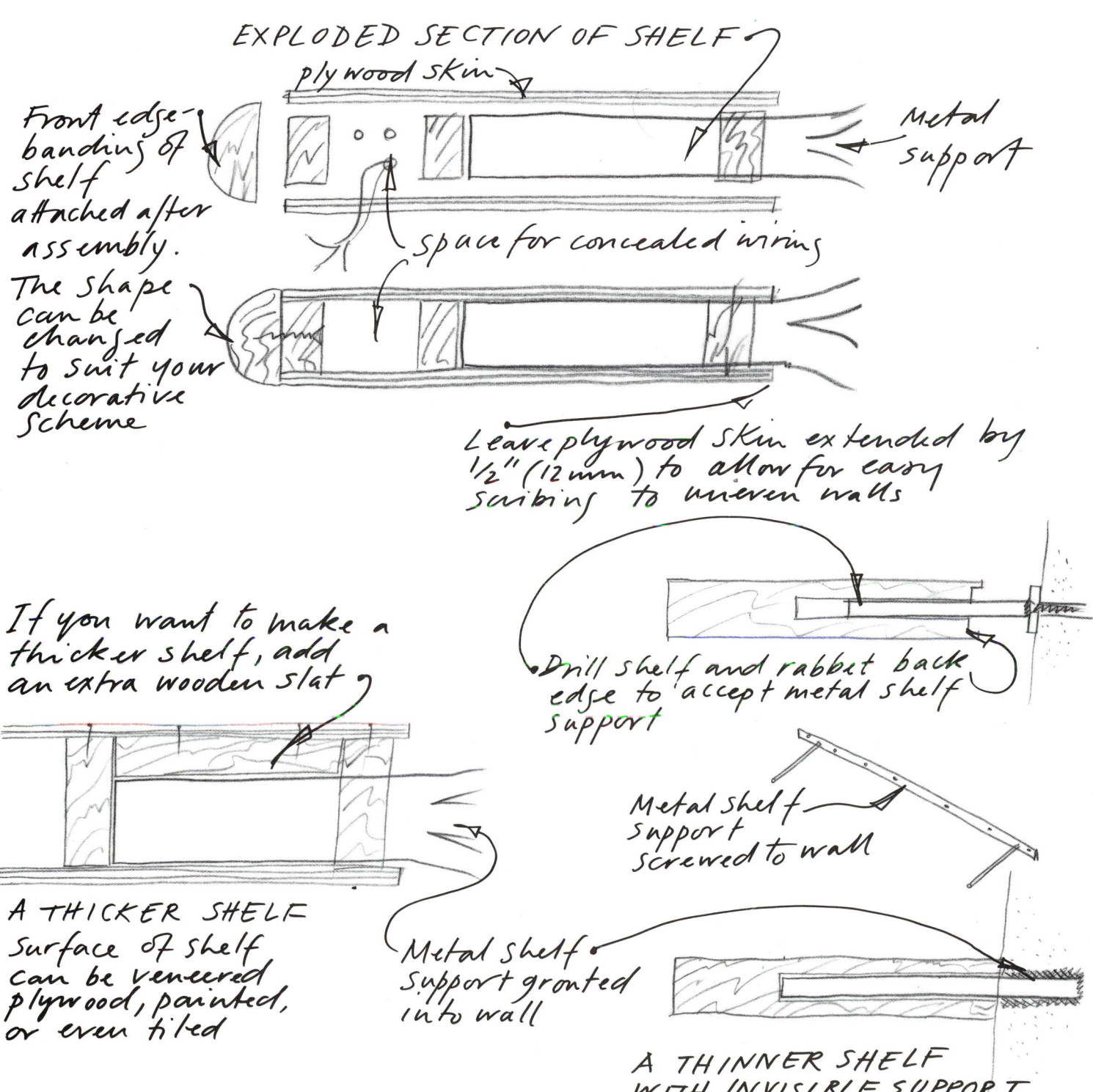

EXPLODED SECTION OF SHELF

plywood skin

Metal support

Front edge-banding of shelf attached after assembly.

The shape can be changed to suit your decorative scheme

space for concealed wiring

Leave plywood skin extended by 1/2" (12mm) to allow for easy scribing to uneven walls

If you want to make a thicker shelf, add an extra wooden slat

A THICKER SHELF
surface of shelf can be veneered plywood, painted, or even tiled

Drill shelf and rabbet back edge to accept metal shelf support

Metal shelf support screwed to wall

Metal shelf support grouted into wall

A THINNER SHELF WITH INVISIBLE SUPPORT

WALL OF DISPLAY SHELVING

This project features shelving without any visible means of support, giving clean lines without any ugly brackets. It is all done by making a hollow box-section shelf unit comprising top and bottom plywood-skin panels over a sturdy lumber framework, creating the appearance of a thick, solid shelf.

For added strength on long shelf runs, protruding steel rods are drilled into the rear wall. They slide into the box frame of the shelf. Battens-only attachment can be used for a run of shelving up to 8ft (2440mm) long and 18in (450mm) deep. It is important to note that steel rods should only be driven 3in (75mm) into walls, whether they are solid or hollow. For cavity walls, the rods should not bridge the cavity. If the walls are plasterboard, stud walls, or lath and plaster, then, for strength, the steel rods should be inserted directly into the main vertical timber studs within the wall.

CONSTRUCTION

Decide on the height of your shelves and, using a carpenter's level, mark their position on the wall; continue these lines on to the end walls. Measure for the length and required depth, and for each shelf cut two pieces of $\frac{3}{8}$in (9mm) thick plywood, or $\frac{1}{2}$in (12mm) MDF or particleboard. If the shelves are to be longer than 8ft (2440mm), you will have to butt-joint the lengths and position a batten inside the shelving to support the cut ends.

From 1 × 2in (25 × 50mm) S4S battening, cut one piece to the length of the shelf for the front batten. Cut two end wall battens to the depth of the shelf, less the thickness of the front batten. Cut two back battens to the length of the shelf less twice the thickness of the end batten so that they will fit between the latter. Cut further battens to the shelf depth, less three batten thicknesses, to fit between the front and back shelf battens at each end and at about 24in (610mm) intervals along its length.

Lay out all the pieces in place on the top panel of the shelf to make sure that they fit together.

Attach some scrap pieces of wood to the underside of the top shelf panel for the steel rods to rest on. These pieces should be of a suitable thickness (about $\frac{3}{4}$in [19mm]) to allow the rods to fit roughly midway in the edges of the back battens. Cut the pieces, if necessary, to fit in between the cross battens inside the shelf, and glue them to the top panel. They will need to be at intervals of about 24in (610mm) to coincide with the steel rod positions (16in [400mm] if you are fitting into a stud wall).

Draw a guide line the thickness of the scrap wood on to the back batten to help positioning when you are drilling steel rod back battens.

The rods should be spaced about every 24in (610mm) (16in [400mm] if drilling into wood studs) roughly midway between the cross battens. They should run the width of the shelf from front to back, butting up against the inner side of the front batten and going into the wall about 3in (75mm) beyond the thickness of the plaster. Cut the required number from $\frac{1}{2}$in (12mm) steel rod.

Clamp the two back battens together, and using a drill bit slightly larger in diameter than the steel rod (an approx. $\frac{9}{16}$in [13mm] drill bit and $\frac{1}{2}$in [12mm] diameter steel rod), drill through the two battens together in the appropriate places. Use a pencil to number the battens.

Nail up the internal frame of the shelf, marking the side to be fixed to the upper panel. Spread glue on the top side of the frame and lay the top shelf panel in place. Draw a line around the edges of the frame and the shelf panel to mark a center line

TOOLS

- STEEL MEASURING TAPE
- CARPENTER'S LEVEL
- TRY SQUARE
- SMALL HAND SAW (or power circular saw or Saber saw)
- HACKSAW
- POWER DRILL or HAND BRACE
- TWIST DRILL BIT, SPADE BIT, or AUGER BIT
- MASONRY DRILL BIT
- HAMMER
- SCREWDRIVER (Phillips or slotted, according to screws used)
- TWO C-CLAMPS
- NAILSET
- SMOOTHING PLANE
- POWER FINISHING SANDER (or hand-sanding block)
- METAL FILE

MATERIALS

Part	Quantity	Material	Length
SHELF PANELS	2	$\frac{3}{8}$in (9mm) plywood or $\frac{1}{2}$in (12mm) MDF or particleboard – width as required	As required
FRONT BATTEN	1	1 × 2in (25 × 50mm) S4S lumber	As shelf length
END WALL BATTENS	2	1 × 2in (25 × 50mm) S4S lumber	Width of shelf, less thickness of front batten
BACK BATTENS	2	1 × 2in (25 × 50mm) S4S lumber	Length of shelf, less twice the thickness of end battens
INTERMEDIATE BATTENS	As required to fit at 24in (610mm) intervals along shelf length	1 × 2in (25 × 50mm) S4S lumber	Shelf width, less three batten thicknesses
ROD SUPPORT BLOCKS	As above	1 × 2in (25 × 50mm) S4S lumber	About 12in (300mm)
STEEL ROD SHELF SUPPORTS	One per 24in (610mm) length of shelf run	$\frac{1}{2}$in (12mm) diameter mild steel rod	Distance from inner side of front batten to back of shelf, plus plaster thickness, plus 3in (75mm)
SHELF FRONT EDGE (rounded)	1	2 × 3in (50 × 75mm) S4S lumber	As shelf length

BASIC ASSEMBLY

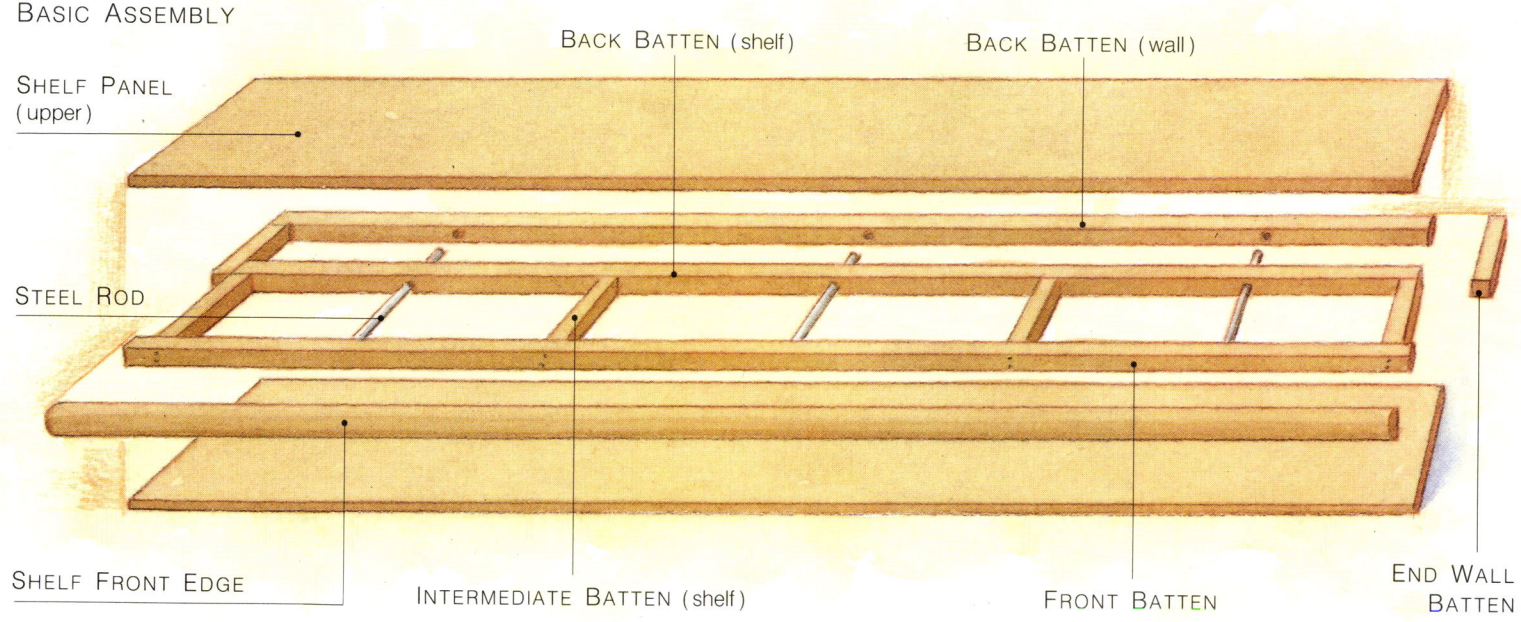

SHELF PANEL (upper)

BACK BATTEN (shelf)

BACK BATTEN (wall)

STEEL ROD

SHELF FRONT EDGE

INTERMEDIATE BATTEN (shelf)

FRONT BATTEN

END WALL BATTEN

of the inset battens to give a nailing line. Nail the panel in place, punch in nail heads and fill the indentations. Repeat for the other shelf panel.

To make a rounded edge at the front, cut a piece of 2 × 3in (50 × 75mm) lumber to the length of the shelf. Glue and nail it (along the

center line) to the front edge, and punch the nail heads well below the surface. Mark a half-round curve on the ends using a suitable plastic cup or carton. Continue rough guide lines on to the top face so that you can use a circular saw to take off the corner edges before planing.

INSTALLING THE SHELF

Screw and anchor the rear-wall batten in place. Then, using a $\frac{1}{2}$in (12mm) diameter masonry drill bit, drill through the pre-drilled holes in the wall batten, making the holes in the bricks or blocks about 3in

(75mm) deep. Screw the end battens against the rear-wall batten.

Bevel both ends of the steel rods with a metal file, then push the rods into the holes in the wall. Slot the shelf on to the protruding rods and slide it over the end battens and on to the rear-wall batten.

① **Stages in Assembling the Box-section Shelf Unit** The basic framework nailed up; holes for steel rods between battens.

② The rear-wall and side battens fit neatly into the recess created by insetting the side and back shelf battens. Holes for rods match up.

③ The lower shelf panel is attached and the upper shelf panel exploded away to show how the softwood frame is neatly recessed.

④ Front edge is attached to front batten and it is rounded off. Through-section (5) shows steel rod resting between support blocks.

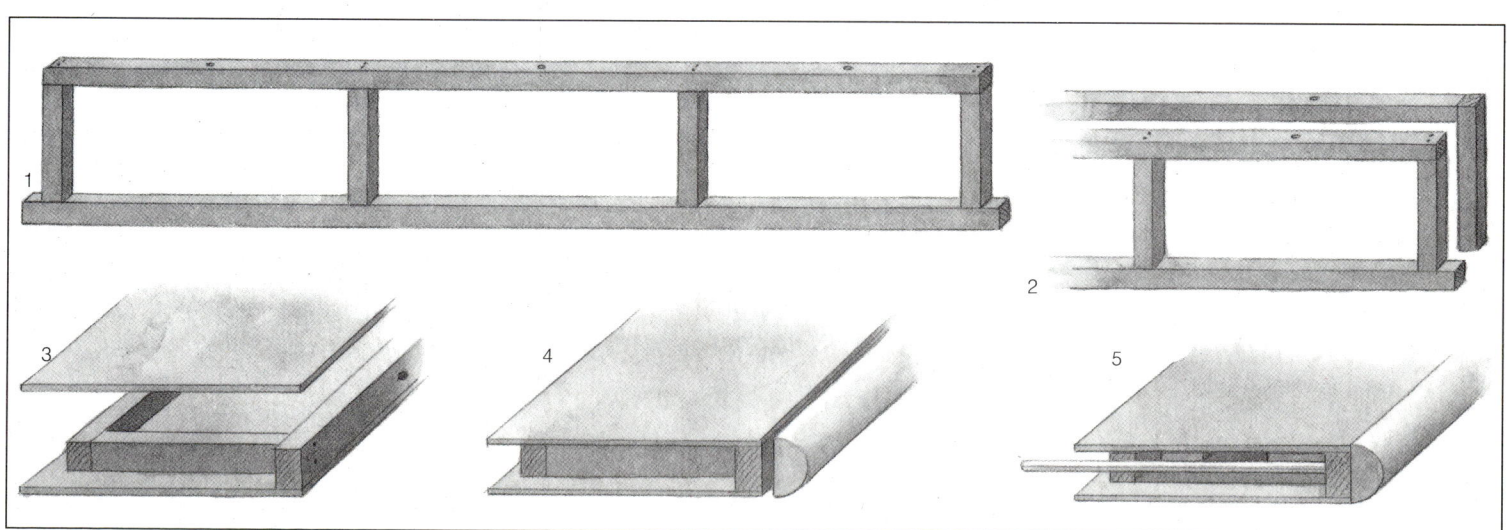

WORKBENCH AND TOOL CUPBOARD

This is the starting point for all serious do-it-yourself enthusiasts. If you make this well it will lead you to undertake many other projects. You will also have a solid bench to work on and practical, safe storage for your tools – two ingredients that will make your work more enjoyable, comfortable, and efficient.

The workbench should be made first. For simplicity, I have used a ply-covered fire-door with a solid lumber core; this is just as tough as the conventional solid beech top used for most professional benches, but is much cheaper. The frame is made from pine, and houses a plywood shelf for large pieces of equipment. A woodworker's vise and retractable stop for planing have been fitted to the bench.

The tool cupboard is secured to the wall with beveled battens, and its two wings (which double as doors) are fitted with locks, and fold back against the wall when the cupboard is in use. It is essential to incorporate lockable doors on a tool cupboard, especially in a household such as mine, where tools vanish with unfailing regularity. All your tools, attachments, nails, and screws have their own storage area and are easily visible, so there is no excuse not to return them to their rightful place when your work is finished; searching around for missing tools never fails to upset the enjoyment of woodwork.

Work lamps are clamped to the top of the cupboard to provide sufficient light where it is most needed, and the gap behind the cupboard allows wiring to be installed for electrical outlets.

Several coats of clear, shiny varnish were applied to the cupboard to give it a thoroughly professional look. Enjoy it and use it well.

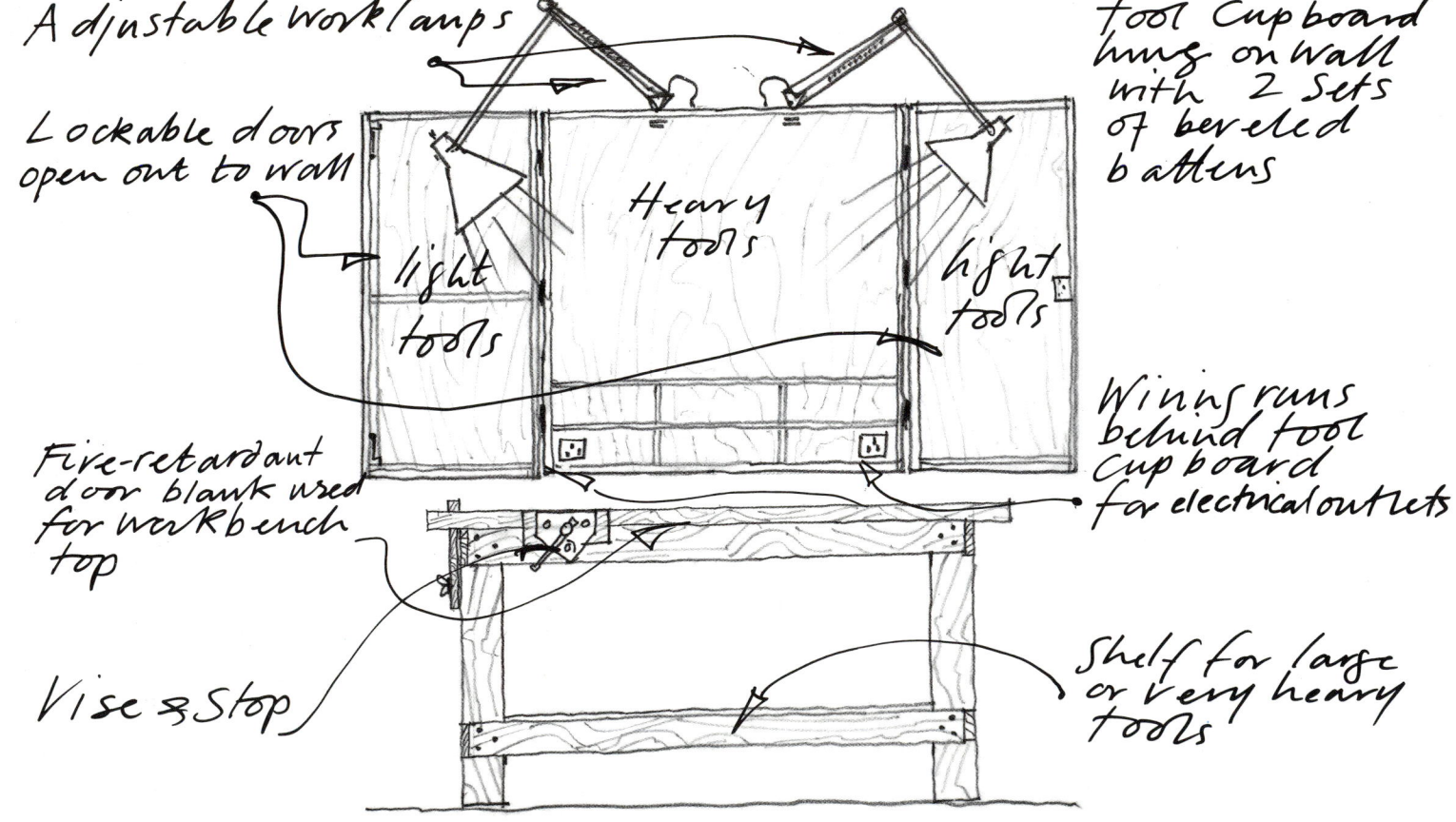

Adjustable work lamps

tool Cupboard hung on wall with 2 sets of beveled battens

Lockable doors open out to wall

light tools

Heavy tools

light tools

Fire-retardant door blank used for workbench top

Wiring runs behind tool Cupboard for electrical outlets

Vise & Stop

Shelf for large or Very heavy tools

WORKBENCH

A sturdy woodworking bench helps you to achieve good results, and constructing your own will provide valuable woodworking experience.

For a neat and solid construction, the top and bottom rails are rabbeted into the bench legs. To speed up and simplify the job, omit the rabbets and simply glue and screw the rails to the sides of the legs, using a woodworking adhesive.

The top of the workbench is a solid-core, fire-retardant flush door blank measuring 6ft 8in × 24in (2050 × 610mm). The top should overhang the frame — by 4in (100mm) at each end, by ½in (12mm) at the back and by at least 1in (25mm) at the front. The overhang allows enough space for C-clamps to hold items to the bench top. The overall height of the bench is 37in (940mm), a comfortable working height for a person about 6ft (1.8m) tall. Decide what is a comfortable working height for you, and adjust the leg lengths accordingly.

The rail lengths are dependent on the size of the door blank used, to give the overhangs mentioned

MATERIALS

Part	Quantity	Material	Length
LEGS	4	6 × 6in (150 × 150mm) S4S softwood	35½in (902mm)
TOP RAILS	2 long 2 short	2 × 6in (50 × 150mm) S4S softwood	To suit door size
BOTTOM RAILS	2 long 2 short	1 × 6in (25 × 150mm) S4S softwood	To suit door size
BENCH TOP	1	Solid core, fire-retardant flush door blank	6ft 8in × 24in (2050 × 610mm)
BENCH TOP BATTENS	2	2 × 2in (50 × 50mm) S4S softwood	Length of the sides between the legs
SHELF	1	½in (12mm) AC grade plywood	As above
BENCH VISE	1		
HANGING BARS	2	1in (25mm) dowel	To suit bench width

TOOLS

FOLDING PORTABLE WORKBENCH/VISE

UTILITY KNIFE

STEEL BENCH RULE

TRY SQUARE

HAND SAW

BACK SAW

CHISEL about ¾in (19mm) wide bench type

CHISEL about 1in (25mm) wide firmer type

DRILL (hand or power)

TWIST DRILL BITS

COUNTERSINK BIT

MARKING GAUGE

ROUTER (an alternative to a chisel for cutting rail rabbets)

above. Whether or not you rabbet the rails into the legs will also affect the length of the rails. The long rails fit inside the shorter end ones. If you rabbet the rails, note that the top rails are thicker than the bottom ones. So the top rails will be shorter than the bottom rail lengths by the difference in thickness between the two rails.

SPADE BIT to make cut-out for bench stop, and holes for hanging bars

TWIST DRILL BIT to make holes for bench-stop bolt

SABER SAW (or compass saw or coping saw) to make vise cut-out

MALLET

BAND CLAMP (or rope and scrap of wood to make tourniquet)

SCREWDRIVER (Phillips or slotted, depending on screw type)

SMOOTHING PLANE

SANDING BLOCK and SANDING PAPER

WRENCH to fit coach screws to install vise

MARKING THE LEGS

Mark the legs to length, squaring the cutting line on all faces, and then cut the legs. Check they are of identical length by standing them together and comparing their heights.

If the rails are to be rabbeted into the legs, mark out the rabbets (see **Techniques, page 82**).

MARKING FOR TOP RAIL

Line up one of the short rails flush with the top of the leg to mark off the depth of the rabbet. Line up a try square underneath to mark off the line squarely. Score a line on to the leg with a utility knife. Mark all four faces of the leg (see **Techniques, page 80**).

1 **Marking and Making the Leg Rabbets for Rails**
Left Mark rabbets for the top and bottom rails. *Center* Top rabbets are cut with a back saw; bottom rabbets with a back saw and chisel. *Right* The leg rail after rabbeting has been done.

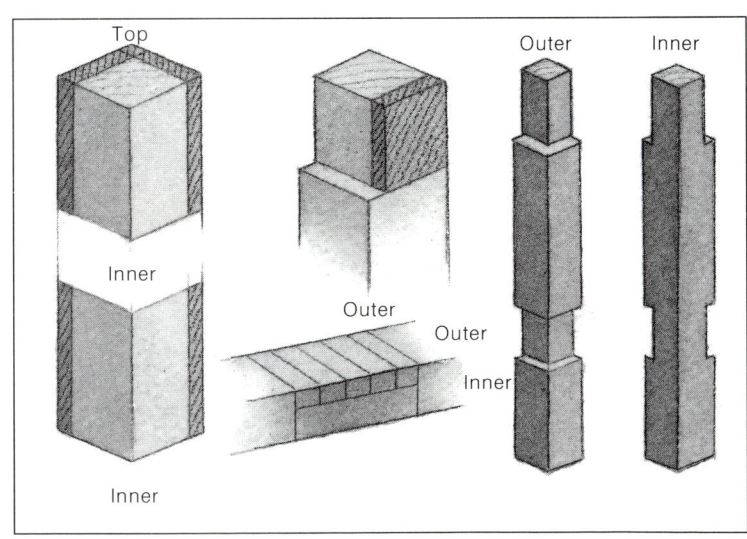

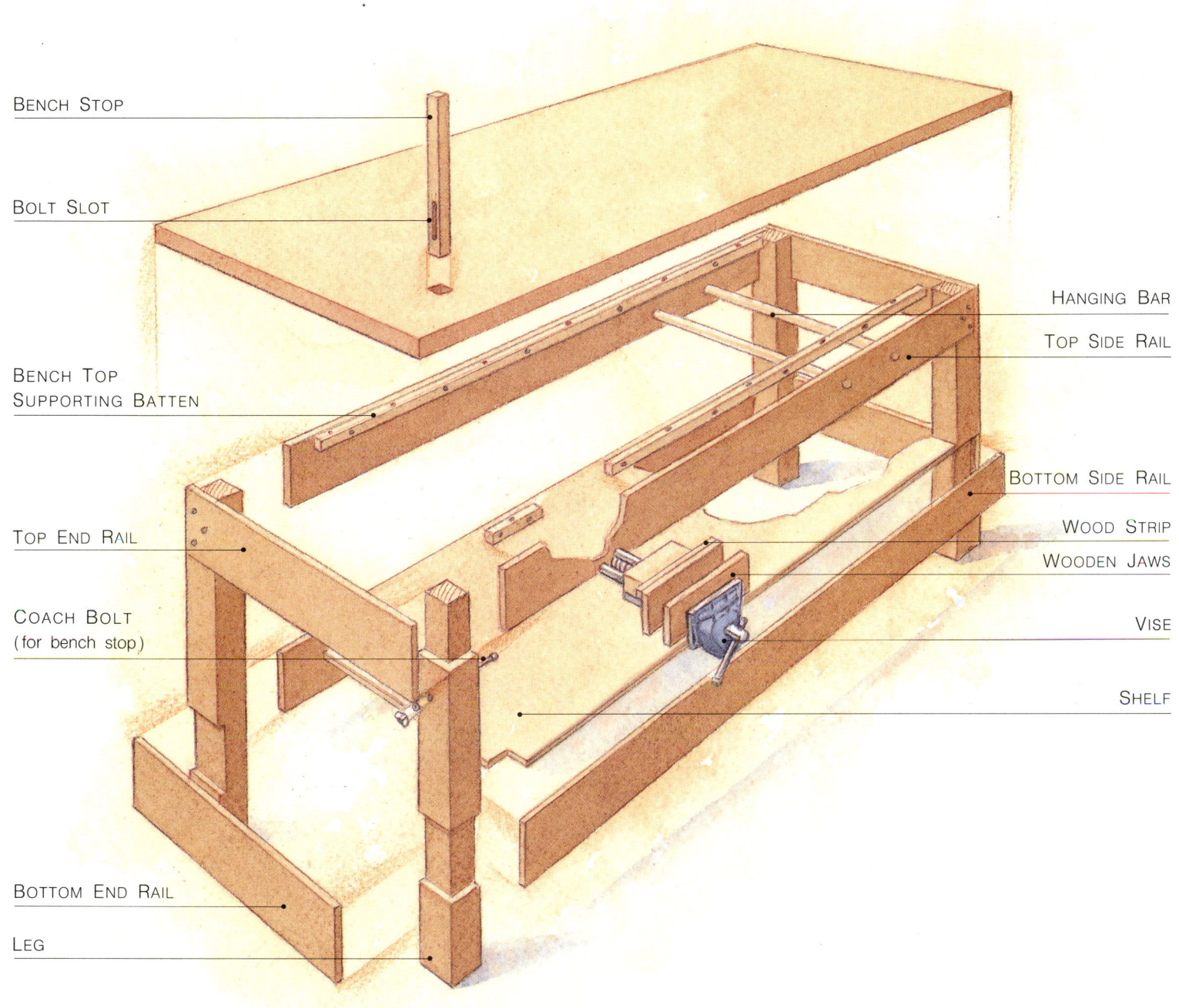

BENCH STOP

BOLT SLOT

BENCH TOP
SUPPORTING BATTEN

TOP END RAIL

COACH BOLT
(for bench stop)

BOTTOM END RAIL

LEG

HANGING BAR

TOP SIDE RAIL

BOTTOM SIDE RAIL

WOOD STRIP

WOODEN JAWS

VISE

SHELF

WORKBENCH

Set the marking gauge to the thickness of the top rail and mark this off on to the top, inner and outer faces of the leg, as shown (fig 1, page 52). Repeat the whole procedure for the other three legs.

MARKING LEG FOR BOTTOM RAIL

For the top of this rail to finish 14in (350mm) from the ground, measure this distance up the leg and mark with a pencil. Put the rail in place underneath and line up your try square underneath. Remove the rail and score a line with a utility knife for the position of the bottom of the rail. Replace the rail against the try square, then move the square to the top of the rail. Remove the rail again and score a line with a utility knife for the position of the top of the rail. Lining up in this way ensures greater accuracy. Continue lines round to the other three faces.

Re-set the marking gauge to the thickness of the lower rail and mark this thickness off on to the inner and outer faces of the legs as shown (fig 1, page 52).

CUTTING FOR TOP RAIL

Hold the leg in a portable workbench or clamp it to a solid table or saw horse and, cutting on the waste side of the line, make the horizontal cuts first, using a back saw to the marked depths. Then make the vertical cuts, using a back or hand saw, on both the outer faces. Remove any waste with a chisel. Alternatively, use a router, with the depth set to the thickness of the rails.

Repeat this procedure for the other three legs.

CUTTING OUT FOR BOTTOM RAIL

Make horizontal cuts with a back saw on the outer faces of one leg at the top and bottom of the rail position, to your marked depths. To cut out the rabbet, make a series of cuts with a back saw down to the marked depths, about $\frac{1}{2}$in (12mm) apart; then pare out the waste with a bench chisel and a mallet (*see* **Techniques, page 82**).

Repeat for the other three legs until the surface is flat.

END FRAME ASSEMBLY

The rails must fit tightly. If necessary, make the rabbet so that they are fractionally undersized and plane down the rails slightly until they fit tightly in the rabbets.

Apply glue to the leg rabbets and position the bottom rail, so that it is flush with the sides. Drill and countersink through the rail into the legs and screw them together with 2in (50mm) No 10 screws – three on each leg. Repeat at the top for the top rail, gluing and screwing as before, using 2½in (65mm) No 10 screws.

Repeat the whole procedure for the second end frame. If you want to simplify construction by not using rabbets, simply glue and screw the rails to the face of the legs. However, make sure that the frames are assembled square, and that the rails overhang the legs by the thickness of the rail.

Clean up, plane, and bevel all the outer edges, then remove any excess glue and sand down all the surfaces for a smooth finish.

ADDING THE LONG RAILS

Stand the two end frames upright and fit the bottom long rails in place, gluing the leg rabbets as before. Remember that the tighter the legs fit, the stronger the frame will be. For a sturdy frame, the shoulders must be pulled up tightly before screwing them together. To do this, use either a band clamp or a rope tourniquet around the frame at the height of the rail joints. If using rope, loop a thin piece of wood in the rope on each side and twist it around to make the frame secure.

Glue and fit the top rails and then tighten them together with a clamp or a rope tourniquet.

Pilot-drill and screw through the rails into the legs in three places, as with the end frames. Once the rails have been screwed, the clamp can be removed.

Clean up, and bevel the top and bottom edges of the bottom rails and the bottom edges of the top rails. Sand down the framework and plane the top of the framework and the top rail flush.

1 **Assembling the Workbench End Frame**
Lay the legs on a flat surface and check that bottom rail fits tightly into the rabbet. Glue and screw in place. Attach top rail in a similar way, then repeat for the legs at the other end.

2 **Adding the Side Rails and Supporting Battens**
Glue and nail the bottom side rails into the leg rabbets first, then repeat for the top rails. In each case hold the frame tightly together with a rope tourniquet to keep it square. *Inset* Corner detail.

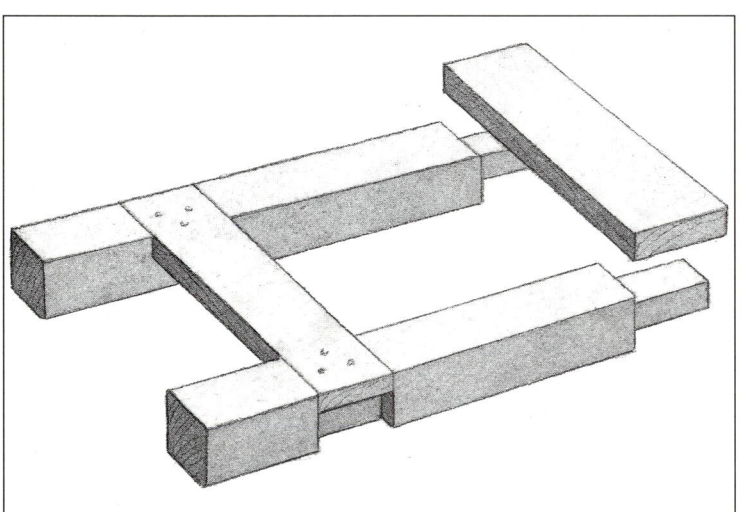

SECURING THE BENCH TOP

Take two battens of 2 × 2in (50 × 50mm) S4S, cut to the length of the sides between the legs. Drill and countersink the battens on two adjacent faces for screws to secure the side and top (ours had five along the side, six along the top). Choose the best side of the frame as the front. At the back, clamp one of the battens in place to the inside of the frame, flush with the top of the top rail, and screw through the side into the rail. The front batten is attached after installing the vise.

Put the top in place, equalizing the overhang each end and allowing ½in (12mm) overhang at the back, and the remainder at the front (enough to take a cramp). Do not screw the top down yet.

INSTALLING A VISE

You will need a vise that fits into the top rail. There is a wide range of woodworking vises to choose from. All have wide-opening jaws and are designed to fit to the underside of the bench top, on the front edge close to a leg, so that the top edge of the jaws (after the lining has been fitted — see below) is level with the bench top. Some smaller vises simply clamp on to the underside of the workbench, but it is best to use one that is designed to be bolted in place. A square body seating will ensure easy fitting to the bench top.

Choose the largest vise you can afford – a jaw opening of about 13in (330mm) is ideal but maximum openings range from 4½in (115mm) up to about 15in (380mm). The larger vises often have a useful quick-release mechanism which allows you to pull the jaw out and in without having to wind the handle as with a normal vise. Make sure that the body of the vise and the sliding jaw have holes to take the plywood liners which protect the work, the vise, and your tools.

The method of fitting varies slightly according to the make of vise chosen, but this is how we installed ours. Remember that the top of the steel jaws must finish a little way down from the worktop, say ½in (12mm), to allow for a wooden strip, which is part of the jaw liners, to be fitted easily.

Measure the depth of the vise. Subtract from this the thickness of the worktop, minus ½in (12mm) (see fig 3). You will need a shim (cut from a scrap of wood) of the same thickness to go under the bench top and to fit between it and the vise.

MAKING THE CUT-OUT FOR THE VISE IN THE SIDE RAIL

You will first need to make a template of the vise. Put the vise on end with its shim and draw around it on to a piece of thick paper or card. Simplify the lines of the template to make cutting the side rail easier. Cut out the template and hold it to the underside of the bench top, about 12in (300mm) in from the front left hand for a right-handed person (or from the right for a left-handed person), and draw around the template on the top rail.

To make the cut-out, remove the bench top, and cut around the line with a power Saber saw or by hand with a compass saw or coping saw.

Clamp the second bench top supporting batten in place to the front top rail as before (see **Securing the Bench Top, left**) and screw it in place, cutting out the section where the gap has been left for the vise with a compass saw or coping saw. Screw the top back in place through the battens.

Slide the vise into position, with the shim in place. Drill pilot holes up through the fixing holes in the bottom of the vise, through the shim, and into the worktop. Secure the vise tightly in place using lag screws and washers.

MAKING THE WOODEN JAW LINERS

The liners are wooden pieces attached inside the jaws of the vise so as to finish flush with the top of the bench. They serve to protect work while it is being held in the vise.

From ½in (12mm) plywood, cut two pieces slightly longer than the steel jaws of the vise. The width of the plywood should equal the distance between the top of the bench and the runner of the vise.

Cut a piece of scrap hardwood to the same thickness as the distance between the top of the steel jaws and the top of the worktop, and to the same length as that of the wooden jaw liners. Glue in place to the front edge of the bench, flush with the worktop, so that it rests on the vise.

ATTACHING THE REAR WOODEN JAW LINER

Mark through the holes in the front of the vise on to one of the wooden jaw liners. Transfer the marks to the other line. Drill and countersink the liners at these marks and screw into the worktop through these holes and the holes in the vise back.

ATTACHING THE FRONT WOODEN JAW LINER

Close the vise with the front wooden jaw clamped in place, and screw through the front holes into the jaw.

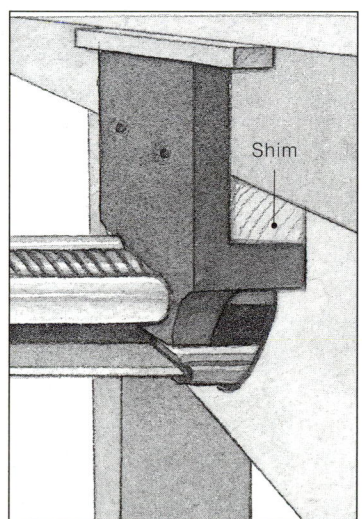

③ Fitting the Bench Vise
Thickness of shim is depth of vise, less thickness of worktop minus the wooden strip.

Shim

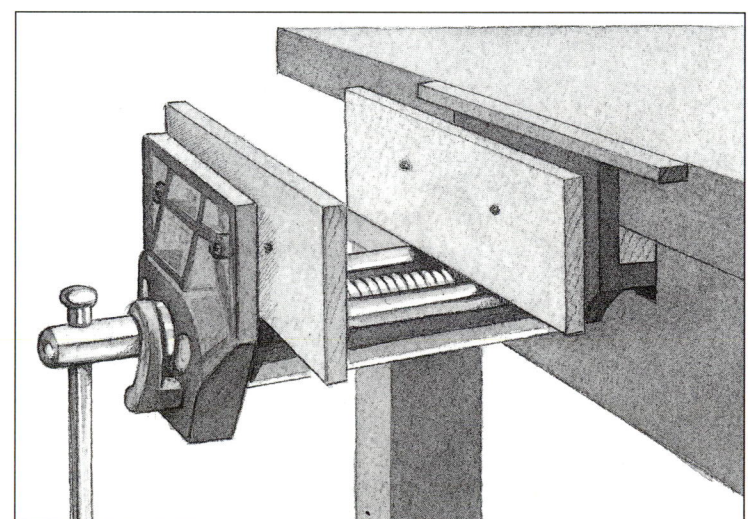

④ Fitting the Wooden Jaw Liner to the Vise
Jaw liners (made from ½in [12mm] plywood) finish flush with the bench top. The rear jaw liner is fixed by screwing it into the worktop. Screw through the front of the vise to attach the front liner.

WORKBENCH

THE BENCH STOP

A bench stop which can be raised above the bench top is useful for pushing against while large pieces of work are planed or chiseled.

The bench stop fits just outside and tangent to the front leg at the vise end. To mark the position of the bench stop on the bench top, square around from the outer edge of the leg using a pencil and try square. The line should be continued from underneath, up the front edge, and on to the top of the workbench. Measure back from the front edge to coincide with the leg. Square off the line from the side with a try square.

Take a piece of hardwood batten about 1 × 1½in (25 × 38mm) and cut to about 10–12in (250–300mm) long. Mark around the end of the batten in position behind the pencil marks on the worktop as shown: that is, to the *outside* of them. Check that the lines will allow the bench stop to fit alongside the leg. Go over the pencil marks with a utility knife.

Using a spade bit as near as possible in size to (but smaller than) the bench top cut-out, drill right through the worktop. Clamp a piece of packing underneath the hole, so that you can then pare out the edges down on to the packing, to avoid breaking the wood underneath. Take care to pare out fractionally *within* the line. Check occasionally with a try square that you are cutting down square. Keep cleaning out until the batten slots into the hole, but stop when the fit is still fairly tight.

INSTALLING BENCH STOP

We used a 6in (150mm) long, ⅜in (9.5mm) diameter carriage bolt with a washer and a wing nut. Mark where the bolt is to be on the leg. (This must be far enough down to clear the top rail.) Fit the stop in place flush with the top. Transfer the bolt mark on to the bench stop – this will be the top of the slot. Move the stop up to the highest position required, that is, about 3–4in (75–100mm), and mark off the bolt position for the bottom of the slot.

Take the bench stop out. Mark off the center line and drill a line of holes ⅜in (9.5mm) in diameter along the length of the slot, with a shim held underneath. Clean out the slot with a chisel until the bolt slides freely inside. Alternatively, use a router to make the slot.

At the marked line on the leg, mark a vertical line in the exact center of the bench stop position, to make sure that the bolt fits in the middle of it. Use a ⅜in (9.5mm) drill bit to drill right through the leg at this point. Slide the stop into place and push the bolt through from the inside of the leg and through the slot. Secure the screw in place with a washer and a wing nut.

ATTACHING THE SHELF

Measure the outside dimensions of the frame and cut a piece of ½in (12mm) thick plywood to this size. Make notches for the legs by measuring and cutting with a power Saber saw or small hand saw. Clean up and bevel the top edges of the shelf and then slot it in place on the bottom rails.

ATTACHING HANGING BARS

These hanging bars are fitted beween the long rails at the opposite end to the vise, and are very useful for hooking things on, such as C-clamps, a dustpan and brush, a paint tin, and other essential items that you may need close by.

Cut two lengths of 1in (25mm) dowel to the width of the underframe, plus a little extra for planing off afterwards. Mark dowel positions about 12in (300mm) and 24in (600mm) in from each of the rail ends, in the center of both the back and front top rails of the bench.

Using a spade bit of the same diameter as the dowel, drill holes at the marks, through the rails, back and front. Put dowels through the holes, hammering them in after smearing the ends with aliphatic resin glue. Plane off the ends flush with the rails.

THE VISE AND BENCH STOP

Often the vise can be used in conjunction with the stop to hold large items.

① Installing the Bench Stop
Enlarge the line of holes in the stop to form a slot. Slot in bench is formed in the same way.

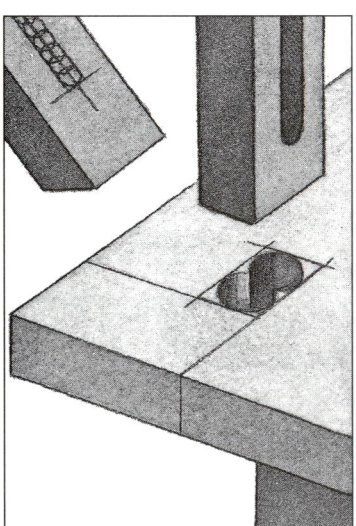

TOOL CUPBOARD

It is important to store tools in a safe and secure place where they are also readily accessible when required. Properly stored tools stay sharp and rust-free, and with each tool in its correct place you will not waste time looking for tools.

This cupboard provides an ideal place to store tools. It is secured to the wall of the workshop or garage where you would normally do home improvements. When the cupboard is in use, the doors open out flat to the wall on each side for easy access to the tools. You can plan it to suit your needs, leaving space for new tools as you buy them.

The rack incorporates outlets for power tools, and adjustable lamps to give excellent illumination of the worksurface below. When not in use, the lamps can be pushed out of the way, and the doors closed. For safety, the cupboard is permanently screwed to the wall through beveled battens, and the doors have a lock for security and to keep the tools out of the way of children.

MAIN CUPBOARD SECTION

Cut the back panel by sawing the full sheet of ½in (12mm) plywood in half to form two 48 × 48in (1220 × 1220mm) sheets. Use a circular saw (or hand saw), running the sole plate against a straight batten clamped to the surface of the plywood sheet to ensure a straight cut (see **Techniques, page 81**).

Measure the exact height of the back panel and cut two pieces of 1 × 4in (25 × 100mm) lumber to this length to form the side rails. Glue and screw these rails on-edge to the back panel with screws about every 9in (230mm), through from the back. Use 1in (25mm) No 8 screws.

Cut two pieces of 1 × 4in (25 × 100mm) lumber about 48in (1220mm) long for the top and bottom rails. Position the pieces and mark off the internal lengths. Cut them squarely to fit between the side rails. Glue and screw these pieces in place on to the back panel as with the side rails. Using 2in (50mm) No 8 screws, attach the sides to the top and bottom rails by inserting two screws into each corner joint.

Finish by removing excess glue and planing any protruding edges. Sand smooth.

DOOR SECTIONS

The door front panels are formed by cutting the remaining 48 × 48in (1220 × 1220mm) panel in half to form two 24 × 48in (610 × 1220mm) panels. The waste incurred by cutting provides the curf (the gap between the two doors).

Cut two pieces of 1 × 3in (25 × 75mm) lumber to length for the side rails. Glue and screw these in place as with the main section.

Again using 1 × 3in (25 × 75mm) lumber, measure for the top and bottom rails as above, and glue in place between the side rails, screwing through the door front. Insert two screws in each corner to secure the sides to the top and bottom.

ORGANIZING THE INSIDE

The inside of the tool cupboard can be organized to suit your own needs, but, for safety, heavy equipment *must* be in the main cupboard.

MATERIALS

Part	Quantity	Material	Length*
SIDE RAILS	2	1 × 4in (25 × 100mm) S4S lumber	48in (1220mm)
TOP & BOTTOM RAILS	2	As above	As above
CUPBOARD SHELVES	3	As above	As above
MOUNTING BATTENS	2	As above	As above
SHELF DIVIDERS	4	As above	4in (100mm)
DOOR SIDE RAILS	4	1 × 3in (25 × 75mm) S4S lumber	48in (1220mm)
DOOR TOP & BOTTOM RAILS	4	As above	24in (610mm)
BOLT MOUNTING BATTEN	1	As above	48in (1220mm)
SLOTTED SHELVES	2	As above	24in (610mm)
SHELF EDGING STRIPS	3	1 × 1in (25 × 25mm) S4S lumber	48in (1220mm)
CHISEL MOUNTING SLOTS	1	2 × 2in (50 × 50mm) S4S lumber	As above

From 1 sheet of N or A grade ½in (12mm) plywood 8 × 4ft (2.44 × 1.22m)			
BACK PANEL	1		48 × 48in (1200 × 1200mm)
DOOR PANELS	2		24 × 48in (610 × 1220mm)

Also required: Offcuts of planed lumber and plywood to make tool-mounting blocks

*Approximate lengths only – refer to text for actual size

TOOLS

STEEL BENCH RULE

UTILITY KNIFE

TRY SQUARE

CIRCULAR SAW (or hand saw or Saber saw)

DRILL (hand or power)

TWIST DRILL BIT

MASONRY DRILL BIT

SPADE BIT

COUNTERSINK BIT

COPING SAW or POWER SABER SAW to cut blocks to fit tool handles

BACK SAW

TWO C-CLAMPS

SCREWDRIVER (Phillips or slotted, depending on type of screws being used)

SMOOTHING PLANE

SANDING BLOCK and SANDING PAPER

TOOL CUPBOARD

The other safety note concerns electrical outlets. If you put these in as we have, they will be at a convenient working height and the cables serving them can be run neatly in conduit in the gap created behind the cupboard by the beveled battens on which it is mounted. It is most important to ensure that the cupboard is screwed firmly to the wall, and to keep a note of the position of the cable runs if you drill the back panel to mount tools in the future. The same caution must be applied to the wiring of lamps if these are attached to the top of the cupboard.

SHELVES FOR THE MAIN CUPBOARD

Cut the shelves from 1 × 4in (25 × 100mm) lumber to the same length as the top and bottom rails. Work out the position of the shelves by laying the cupboard down and trying equipment in place.

When the shelves are correctly positioned, mark the center line on to the sides, and continue the line on to the back to give a line for the screw positions. Glue the shelves in place and screw through from the back and through the sides.

Decide, according to your requirements, how you want to partition the shelves. For the dividing pieces, measure and cut them to size from the same size of lumber as the shelves. Put the dividers in place and mark around them on the inside of the cupboard. Take the dividers away, and drill through the back panel from the front so that you can see where to screw from the back. Replace the dividers, countersink the fixing holes in the back panel, and then screw through from the back into the dividers.

Nail 1 × 1in (25 × 25mm) battens in place at the front of the shelves to prevent things falling off. Place small strips across the shelves where planes will be positioned so that the plane blades do not rest on them and get damaged.

MOUNTING TOOLS

Some tools, such as power drills and mallets, can be mounted on solid blocks of wood.

Roughly draw around the shape of the handle on to a piece of thick paper, and cut wood to this shape with a Saber saw or coping saw.

To fit the handles in place, screw through from the back using the method for fitting shelf dividers.

For the chisel slots use a piece of 2 × 2in (50 × 50mm) lumber with a row of holes drilled to a diameter smaller than the chisel handles.

Using a spade bit, drill a row of holes through the middle of the block. With a back saw, cut slots in the front as shown to allow the chisel blade to turn in through the slot.

Various springs, clips, and hooks can be used to hold other tools.

SHELVES FOR THE DOORS

These shelves have slots cut in them to a variety of sizes, providing a useful way to store screwdrivers, marking gauges, and other tools that are longer than they are wide.

Drill holes in the middle of the shelves and cut through them from the front to form slots in the same way as with the chisels. Install the shelves as with the main cupboard.

Try squares are held in place by pieces of 1 × 3in (25 × 75mm) lumber rabbeted using a back saw.

ATTACHING THE TOOL MOUNTS

An advantage of this tool cupboard is its versatilty. You can organize it to suit your precise requirements, but leave enough space for more tools to be added later.

1 **Forming the Chisel Slots**
Holes are drilled in 2 × 2in (50 × 50mm) lumber with beveled edge, and slots are cut out.

2 **Making a Saw Holder**
A block of wood shaped to fit inside a saw handle is screwed to a turnbuckle made from plywood or MDF.

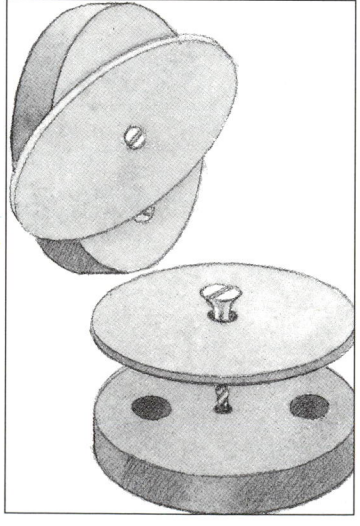

3 **Attaching the Door Hinges**
Doors carry a lot of weight so hinges must be substantial and secured with long screws.

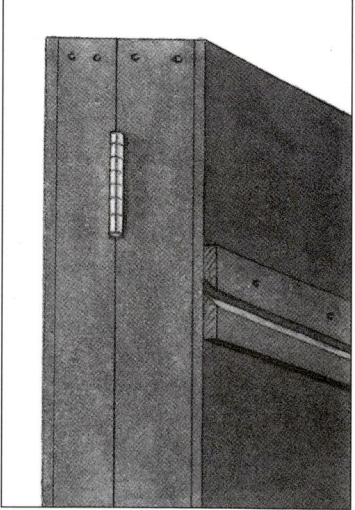

DOOR TOP RAIL

DOOR FRONT

BACK

BACK TOP RAIL

SHELF DIVIDER

SLOTTED SHELF

EDGING BATTEN

SIDE RAIL

DOOR BOTTOM RAIL

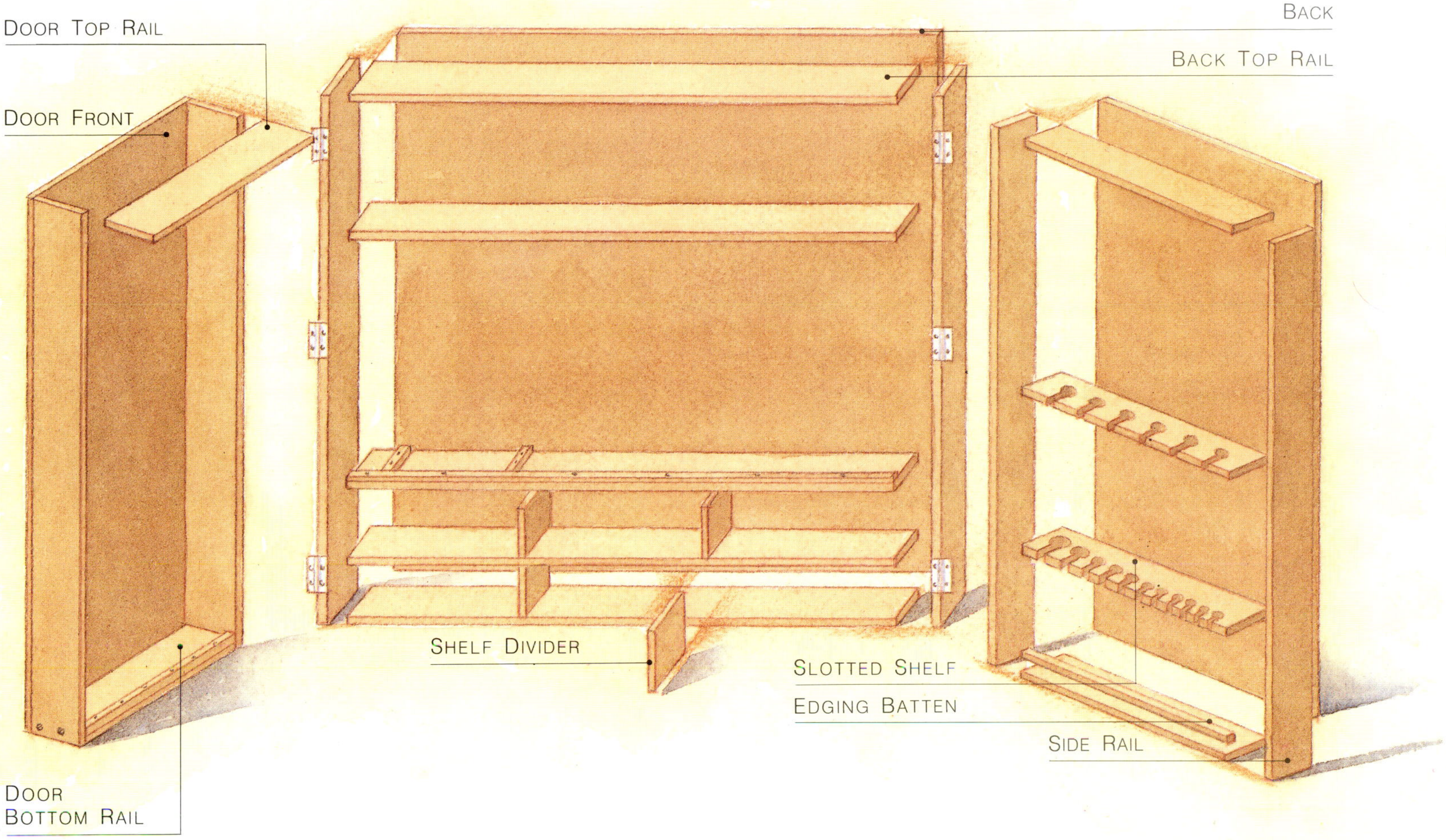

TOOL CUPBOARD ASSEMBLY

MOUNTING SAWS

Tools with open handles, such as saws, can be mounted on shaped blocks of wood fitted with turn-buckles that fit inside the handles.

Use a piece of wood slightly thicker than the handle and draw around the inner shape of the handle on the wood. Cut out the wood to this shape with a Saber saw or coping saw. Cut a piece of $\frac{1}{4}$in (6mm) plywood or MDF to the same shape.

Screw the block to the door using two screws. Screw the turn-buckle to the block with one central screw which is secure but will allow the turn-buckle to turn.

Screw hooks can be placed as necessary in the front doors.

HANGING THE DOORS

Hang the doors on the main cup-board using three butt hinges for each (see **Techniques, page 93**).

The left-hand door is secured with two swan-neck (flush) bolts which fit into catch plates attached to the bottom rail and to the underside of the top shelf (the top rail is not easy to reach). To make it possible to install the bolts, screw a strip of 1 × 3in (25 × 75mm) lumber to the inside edge of the door's side rail. Attach a lock (see **Techniques, page 95**) and door handles.

SECURING TO THE WALL

For safety, the cupboard is hung on beveled battens (see **Techniques, page 85**). Cut two lengths of 1 × 4in (25 × 100mm) lumber to the width of the cupboard. To bevel the bat-tens, cut each piece lengthwise through half of its thickness with the saw blade angled at 45°. The top section is screwed to the cupboard back, and the lower part to the wall.

Screw the top-section battens to the back of the cupboard about 7in (180mm) down from the top, and about 10in (250mm) up from the bottom, using seven 1$\frac{1}{2}$in (38mm) No 10 screws in each.

Put the lower-section battens in place under the top-section battens and measure down from the top to the bottom edge of the lower batten. Decide where the cupboard is to sit on the wall, then measure this dis-tance down and fix the lower batten to the wall at this height with 2$\frac{1}{2}$in (65mm) No 10 screws and anchors.

Measure down and secure the upper batten in the same way, or sit the cupboard on the first batten and mark the wall for the other batten.

Secure the cupboard firmly to the wall by screwing through the back into the lower-section battens. This is most important if electrical outlets are to be installed in the cupboard.

HOME OFFICE

Whether you need a place in which to do your household accounts and other domestic paperwork or whether you earn your living from home (a growing trend in this age of computerization), you will need a quiet, well-organized space that encourages you to get down to work. This design for a home office provides the essential work area, although it cannot, unfortunately, guarantee the necessary peace and quiet.

I have used conventional steel filing cabinets as pedestals for the desk. The cabinets are well engineered to allow the heavy drawers to run smoothly and to lock securely. The wall unit is pigeonholed with adjustable shelves on "magic wires" so all your files, ledgers, and office equipment can be neatly stacked away.

Because the unit is attached away from the wall with beveled battens, there is enough space behind it for wiring-in

power points; these allow for the increasing amount of electronic equipment that modern life deems necessary.

It is important to have light on the worksurface: it allows you to see what you are doing and also invites you to concentrate and work industriously. The light is provided here by a concealed incandescent strip across the full width of the worksurface, illuminating the bulletin board and its memory-jogging messages.

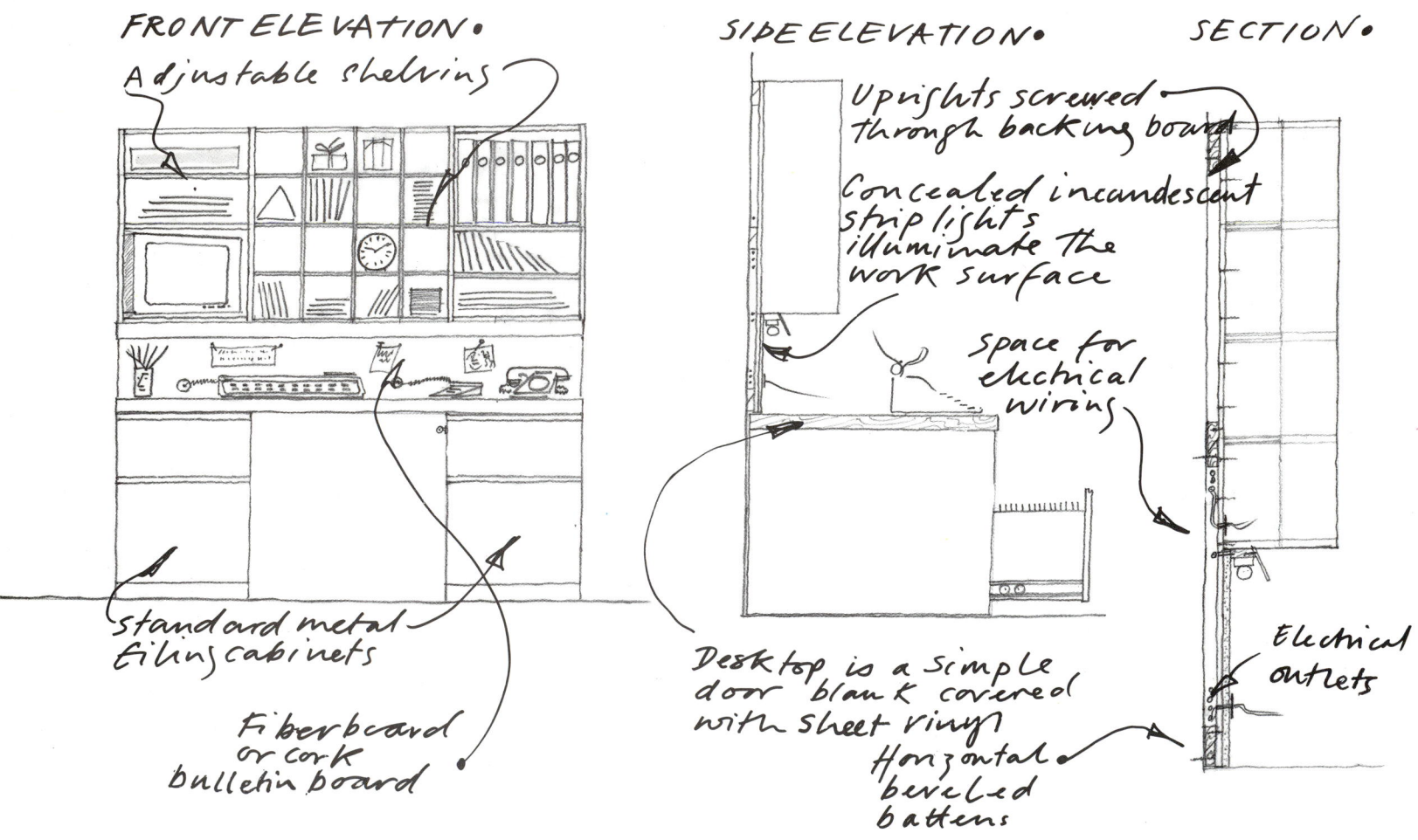

FRONT ELEVATION.
Adjustable shelving

standard metal filing cabinets

Fiberboard or cork bulletin board

SIDE ELEVATION.
Uprights screwed through backing board

Concealed incandescent strip lights illuminate the work surface

space for electrical wiring

Desktop is a simple door blank covered with sheet vinyl

Horizontal beveled battens

SECTION.

Electrical outlets

HOME OFFICE

This project offers an easy way to create office space in the home. The desk could not be simpler – it is just a flush door laid across a couple of two-drawer filing cabinets. At the back of the desk a bulletin board is fixed to the wall, and above it is a boxed unit of adjustable pigeon-holes. These are very adaptable as they are supported by Swedish-type shelf supports. This means their heights can be altered easily and sections can be removed or interchanged to take office equipment, materials, books, and so on.

To give a good, general-purpose working light, strip lights are concealed behind a valance fitted to the bottom of the shelf unit. Electrical outlets and a telephone jack can be installed in the bulletin board section to allow a desk lamp, word processor or typewriter, telephone, and other equipment to be connected. Also incorporated in the design are two conduit covers, drilled through the center of the bulletin board to take cables serving the keyboard and printer through to the back of the unit where they will be hidden.

There is quite a bit of wiring behind this unit. Therefore, both the wall unit and the bulletin board are mounted on beveled battens, which not only give a strong support, but also form a gap for the wiring.

If you do not want to hide the wires behind the unit, and the backing wall is solid, with sound plaster, then you can mount the wall unit and the bulletin board directly on the wall by screwing through the back panel into anchors. In this case, the screwheads will show, so for neatness either fit screw cups under the screwheads or alternatively fit screw covers over them.

The main benefit of this wall unit is that it can be attached to any wall to create an instant study or office, whether in the corner of a living room or in a spare bedroom.

TOOLS

- STEEL MEASURING TAPE
- STEEL BENCH RULE or STRAIGHT-EDGE
- TRY SQUARE
- ADHESIVE SPREADER
- UTILITY KNIFE
- POWER CIRCULAR SAW (or power Saber saw)
- DRILL (hand or power)
- MASONRY DRILL BIT to suit size of anchors used
- TWIST DRILL BIT for clearance holes
- TWIST DRILL BIT for pilot holes and shelf support wire location
- COUNTERSINK BIT
- COMPASS SAW (if Saber saw not available) for cutting recesses for electrical outlets
- ROUTER and ROUTER BIT
- SCREWDRIVER (Phillips or single-slot, depending on the type of screws used)
- ORBITAL SANDER (or hand-sanding block)
- PAINTBRUSH

MATERIALS

Part	Quantity	Material	Length
DESK UNIT			
BASES	2	Two-drawer filing cabinets	
DESK TOP	1	Plywood-faced interior door blank	As required
BULLETIN BOARD			
BACKING BOARD	1	$\frac{1}{2}$in (12mm) plywood or lumber core, 12in (300mm) wide	As desk top
FACING BOARD	1	$\frac{1}{2}$in (12mm) medium fiberboard, 12in (300mm) wide	As desk top
MOUNTING BATTENS	2	1 × 3in (25 × 75mm) S4S lumber	As desk top
WALL UNIT			
BACK PANEL	1	$\frac{1}{2}$in (12mm) plywood or lumber core, 34$\frac{1}{2}$in (870mm) wide	As desk top
SIDE PANELS	2	$\frac{3}{4}$in (19mm) plywood or lumber core, 13in (330mm) wide	34$\frac{1}{2}$in (870mm)
MAIN DIVIDERS	2	$\frac{3}{4}$in (19mm) plywood or lumber core, 13in (330mm) wide*	Distance between top and bottom panels
TOP AND BOTTOM PANELS	2	$\frac{3}{4}$in (19mm) plywood or lumber core, 13$\frac{1}{2}$in (330mm) wide*	Distance between side panels
MIDDLE DIVIDERS	3	$\frac{1}{2}$in (12mm) plywood, 13in (330mm) wide*	Distance between top and bottom panels)
CENTRAL SHELVES	12	$\frac{1}{2}$in (12mm) plywood, 13in (330mm) wide	8in (200mm)
SIDE SHELVES	6	$\frac{1}{2}$in (12mm) plywood, 13in (330mm) wide	Distance between main divider and side
MOUNTING BATTENS	2	1 × 4in (25 × 100mm) S4S lumber	As desk top
VALANCE			
FRONT PANEL	1	$\frac{1}{2}$in (12mm) plywood, 3in (75mm) wide	As desk top
SIDE PANEL	2	$\frac{1}{2}$in (12mm) plywood, 3in (75mm) wide	6in (150mm)
CORNER BLOCK	2	1 × 1in (25 × 25mm) S4S lumber	3in (75mm)

*Approximate lengths only – refer to copy for actual size.

BASIC ASSEMBLY

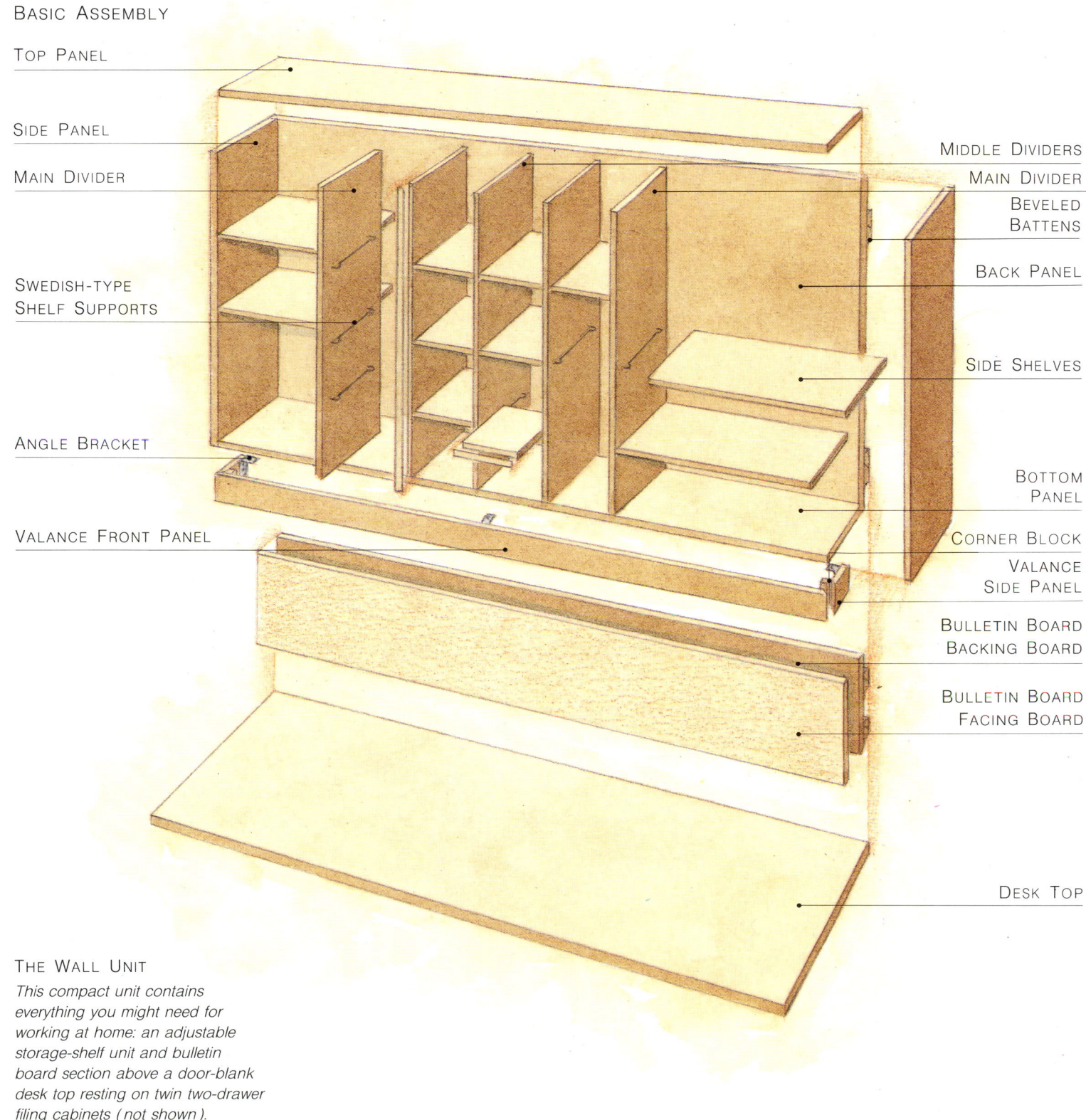

TOP PANEL

SIDE PANEL

MAIN DIVIDER

SWEDISH-TYPE
SHELF SUPPORTS

ANGLE BRACKET

VALANCE FRONT PANEL

MIDDLE DIVIDERS

MAIN DIVIDER

BEVELED
BATTENS

BACK PANEL

SIDE SHELVES

BOTTOM
PANEL

CORNER BLOCK

VALANCE
SIDE PANEL

BULLETIN BOARD
BACKING BOARD

BULLETIN BOARD
FACING BOARD

DESK TOP

THE WALL UNIT

*This compact unit contains
everything you might need for
working at home: an adjustable
storage-shelf unit and bulletin
board section above a door-blank
desk top resting on twin two-drawer
filing cabinets (not shown).*

Home Office: Desk and Wall Unit

Desk

Position the filing cabinets about 40in (1015mm) apart. Place the desk top across them. This can be a plywood-faced interior flush door, finished as required (see **Techniques, page 92**). We covered our door with a sheet of thick sheet vinyl which makes a good writing surface. To stick it in place, use a contact adhesive applied to the upper surface of the door with a serrated spreader. Cut the vinyl slightly oversized, position it carefully, then weight it down overnight to allow the adhesive to harden. Finally, with a utility knife trim off the surplus vinyl at a slight angle to leave a neatly beveled edge.

Bulletin Board

Cut the backing board for the bulletin board from ½in (12mm) plywood or lumber core to the length of the desk top. Our board is 12in (300mm) high, but you can adjust this to suit your requirements.

Cut out the bulletin board itself to the same size. We have used a brand-name finished fiberboard, but you can use any material that will take thumb tacks, such as cork or felt-covered fiberboard. In the latter case, the felt covers the board, front and sides, and is stapled or glued at the back.

Screw the bulletin board to the backing board using flat head wood screws fitted into screw cups for neatness. About four screws at both the top and bottom will be sufficient.

Attaching the Bulletin Board to the Wall

The bulletin board on its backing board is mounted on two pairs of beveled battens. Each pair of battens is made from 1 × 3in (25 × 75mm) S4S (smooth 4 sides) lumber cut to the full length of the bulletin board. Cut through the middle of each length with a circular-saw blade set at 45° to make a pair of beveled battens (see **Techniques, page 85**). Beveled battens allow the bulletin board to fit snugly against the wall, but leave enough space to conceal wiring for lamps, a telephone, and a word processor which sit on top of the desk.

Place the pairs of beveled battens on the back of the bulletin board to position them and screw the upper ones to the back of the bulletin board.

To attach the bulletin board to the wall, first rest it in place at the back of the desk top. This is important as the desk gives extra support for the things above. Hold the lower battens in place under the two fitted ones, and with a pencil mark their positions on the wall.

Take the bulletin board away and, using anchors, screw the lower battens to the wall. Hang the bulletin board on the battens, making sure that the two sets of battens interlock neatly and securely.

Wall Unit

The unit shown here is made from ½in (12mm) lumber core, with an edge-banding applied to the front. Alternatively, you could use ordinary veneered particleboard, with either a wood or a plastic finish, left natural or painted black or a color to suit your decorative scheme.

Using ½in (12mm) plywood, lumber core or veneered particleboard, cut out the back panel to the same length as the desk top and to the desired height; ours is 34½in (870mm) high, which allows for four shelves in the center with a depth of 8in (200mm) each.

Using ¾in (19mm) plywood or lumber core, cut out the side panels, the top and bottom panels, and the two main dividers. The side panels should be the height of the back panel, the top and bottom panels fit between them, and the two main dividers fit between the top and bottom panels. The depth of all these panels is as required – in our case it is 13in (330mm). Add a hardwood molding edge-banding to all the front edges of these panels (see **Materials, page 78**).

Lay the back panel on a flat surface, and place the top, bottom, and side panels in their positions on top of it. Mark these positions on the front of the back panel.

1 Bulletin Board Assembly
Bulletin board is medium fiberboard screwed to plywood or lumber core and hooked over beveled battens.

2 Spacing the Middle and Main Vertical Dividers
Put central divider in place, exactly in center. Use two shelf panels to position the next dividers on each side of the central one. Position all of the dividers in this way.

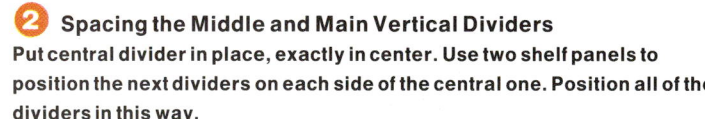

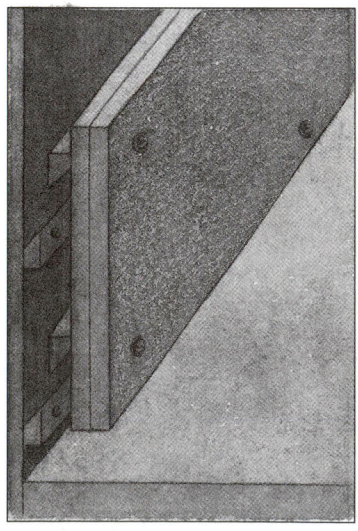

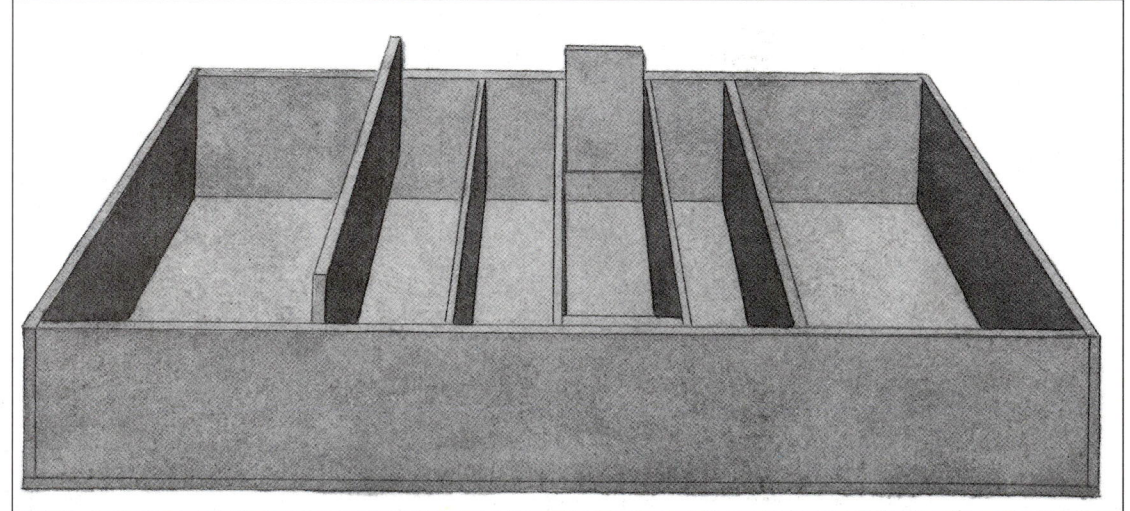

POSITIONING THE DIVIDERS

Your starting point for positioning the dividers will be the position of major items, such as a word processor, that need to be incorporated. Otherwise, you can start with the pigeon-hole section in the middle. This has been planned to provide 16 pigeon-holes 8in (200mm) square – four across by four high.

Cut three middle dividers to the same dimensions as the main dividers, but from $\frac{1}{2}$in (12mm) plywood, lumber core, or veneered particleboard. From the same material, cut 12 shelves, in our case measuring 8×13in (200×330mm). Add edge-banding to the front edges of all the shelves and dividers.

Put the central divider in place, exactly in the center, and mark its position on the back panel. Use two of the shelves to position the next divider on either side of the central one. Then repeat the procedure to position the main dividers. When you have done this, the positions of all the dividers will be marked on the back panel.

SHELVES

Measure the space between the main divider and the side of the wall unit on each side. Using $\frac{1}{2}$in (12mm) plywood, cut shelves to these dimensions and add edge-banding to the front edges. We have three shelves on each side of the main divider.

Position all the shelves with equal spacing between them. Even if some of the shelves are to be left out to accommodate tall books and office equipment, it is still worth buying supports for all of the shelves in case extra shelf space is needed later. When the shelves are correctly positioned, mark their positions on to the sides of the panels and then on to the dividers.

DRILLING THE BACK PANEL

Remove all the panels and shelves, and pilot-drill the back panel through from the front, along the center of the lines marked for the top, bottom, and side panels, and for all the dividers. Turn the panel over and countersink the holes from the back *(see* **Techniques, page 83**).

③ Attaching the Dividers in the Wall Unit Framework
Mark center line of each divider to ensure accurate positioning. Drill, countersink, and screw the divider in place, attaching it securely through the top and bottom panels.

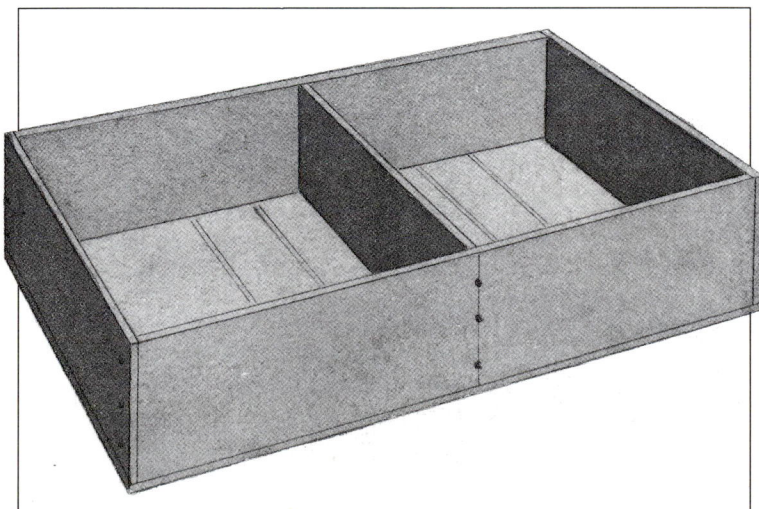

DETAIL OF HOME OFFICE
The bulletin board includes an electrical outlet and a metal disk to house wiring for office equipment. The position of the pigeon-hole shelves can be adjusted to accommodate large items such as a word processor.

HOME OFFICE: WALL UNIT

DRILLING SIDE PANELS AND DIVIDERS

Allowing two per shelf, buy the required number of Swedish-type shelf supports of the appropriate length. Pre-drill the side panels and dividers to take the shelf supports. Positioning the drill on the *center* of the lines marked for the shelves, use a ⅛in (3mm) twist drill bit to drill through the dividers, but drill only ⅜in (9mm) into the side panels. Make sure that the holes at the front of the unit are set back a little from the edge so that the front of the shelf will conceal the shelf support wires. The holes at the back are spaced according to the length of the shelf support wires, to allow the wires to be pushed into the holes.

ASSEMBLING THE OUTER FRAME

Install one side panel by gluing and screwing it from the back.

Drill and countersink holes in the end of the side panel to attach one of the long panels (top or bottom). Glue and screw this panel in place.

Pull the back panel over the edge of the workbench, then screw up from the back into the long panel. Repeat the procedure for the other side panel of the outer frame.

After gluing the ends and rear edge of the other long panel, put it in position and screw through the side panels into the ends. Do not insert screws at the back until you have attached the dividers, so that small adjustments can be made if necessary when the dividers are positioned.

ATTACHING THE DIVIDERS

Apply glue to the ends of the central divider and put it in place, checking with a try square that it is square to the frame and vertical. To ensure accurate positioning of the screws in the ends of the divider, draw a line from the center line of the divider, over the front edges of the long panels, and then across them. Drill, countersink, and screw the divider in place through the long panels. As one panel is not yet attached, it is possible to make adjustments, if necessary, to ensure that the front

edges are flush. Repeat the procedure with the other dividers, working from the center outwards.

Turn the unit over and, working from the back, screw the remaining long panel in place. Finish by screwing through this panel into each of the dividers.

INSTALLING SHELVES

Position the shelf support wires in the dividers. Using a router, make ⅛in (3mm) grooves ⅜in (9mm) deep in the edges of the shelves, so that the shelves will be able to be slotted over the shelf support wires. Make sure that the grooves stop short of the front edges of the shelves, so that the grooves and the wire supports will not be seen.

FINISHING

Fill the screw holes, rub down the filler when dry, and apply your chosen finish (*see* **Techniques, page 80**). The finish should be selected so that it suits the style of the home office and blends in with the decorative scheme you have planned for the room.

ATTACHING THE UNIT TO THE WALL

The unit is hung using two pairs of beveled battens, in the same way as the bulletin board, but with 1 × 4in (25 × 100mm) battens (*see* **Techniques, page 85**). Place the two pairs of battens on the back of the unit to position them, and attach the *top* battens to the back of the unit. It is important to ensure that the fixing screws go through into each upright panel and divider, to give sufficient strength to hold the unit.

To attach the unit to the wall, hold it in place on top of the bulletin board and mark off the positions of the lower battens on the wall, as you did with the bulletin board. Take the unit away and screw the lower parts of the battens to the wall using anchors. Hang the unit in place, making sure that the battens interlock to give a secure fixing.

PIGEON-HOLE SHELF UNIT
The shelves offer ample storage space and are secured firmly to the wall with beveled battens.

1 Hidden Shelf Support
Swedish-type shelf supports "plug" into holes drilled in wall unit dividers; shelf slots over wires.

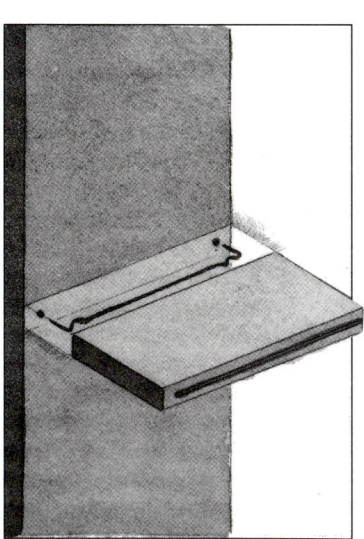

VALANCE

Using $\frac{1}{2}$in (12mm) plywood or lumber core, cut out the valance front to the length of the unit and about 3in (75mm) wide. Cut two side pieces to the same width and about 6in (150mm) long.

Miter the front corners and fit a 1 × 1in (25 × 25mm) batten, cut to the valance depth, to the inside of each corner. Glue and screw it in place to the front and side pieces.

Attach the valance in place to the underside of the bottom of the wall unit using steel angle brackets behind the valance – one at each end and one in the middle.

Install lights behind the valance. We used four tungsten-tube strip lights. The wiring for the lights can be run in the space behind the units created by the bevel of the battens.

It is easy to cut recesses in the bulletin board with a Saber saw or a compass saw to take electrical outlets and a telephone jack. Conduit covers with the centers drilled out can be installed to take the cables for office equipment.

② The Valance Attachment
Valance panels are neatly mitered and screwed to corner blocks. Brackets attach valance to unit.

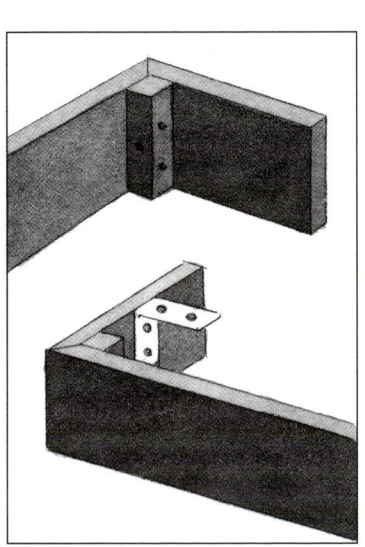

BACK PANEL

BEVELED BATTEN (attached to unit)

BEVELED BATTEN (attached to (wall))

CAVITY

WALL

BEVELED BATTEN
(attached to backing board)

CAVITY
(use for wiring runs)

BACKING BOARD

WALL UNIT
SIDE PANEL

VALANCE
SIDE PANEL

BULLETIN BOARD

DESK TOP

TWO-DRAWER
FILING CABINET

SIDE VIEW OF HOME
OFFICE

WORKROOM IDEAS

ADJUSTABLE SHELVING

To be efficient when working at home you need to be well-organized and comfortable, and that requires careful planning. For both the examples shown here the bulletin board, shelving, and furniture harmonize well with the decorative treatment of walls and floor.

Adequate storage is essential – there is nothing more frustrating than being swamped by paper and unable to find anything. Drawer storage will probably be required and is ideally provided by a deep filing-cabinet-type drawer. You will also need cupboards and lots of shelves, as shown on the right. Here, a sturdy, adjustable shelf system has been combined with bulletin boards for messages and memos.

The shelves are ordinary $\frac{5}{8}$in (15mm) laminated particleboard on adjustable steel shelf supports spaced about 24in (610mm) apart to ensure that the shelves do not sag when heavily loaded.

At the bottom of the adjustable tracks, wide shelf supports are fitted to carry a laminated worktop which provides extra space for storage and working. This standard 24in (610mm) wide worktop, $1\frac{1}{4}$in (30mm) thick, has a hardwood edge-banding and rests on $18\frac{1}{2}$in (470mm) wide supports to which it is screwed from the underside.

Bulletin boards are constructed from $\frac{3}{8}$in (9.5mm) thick medium fiberboard panels cut to fit between the adjustable shelf uprights. The panels are covered in felt which is stapled at the back.

PLAN STORAGE

A simple storage idea is shown in the photograph of the office (opposite). U-shaped brackets support half-round gutters, which store plans and drawings.

Temporarily attach a vertical batten to the wall to align the brackets, and use a carpenter's level to mark horizontal lines for their heights. Space them all equally, marking screw holes on the wall. Drill and anchor to the wall.

1 **Marking Height of Shelving**
Cut uprights to equal length. Hold upright on wall and mark position of the base.

2 **Attach Batten to Wall**
Temporarily nail a batten to the wall to align with marked line. Check that it is level.

3 **Mark Screw Fixing Holes**
Rest upright on temporary batten, check it is vertical, then mark screw hole positions on wall.

4 **Cut Bulletin Board to Shape**
Fit two brackets and double-check they are level. Measure between them; cut bulletin board to fit.

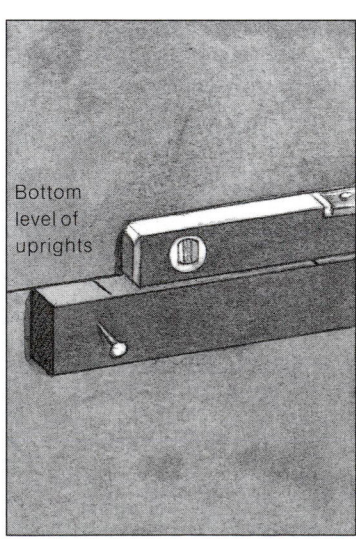

Bottom level of uprights

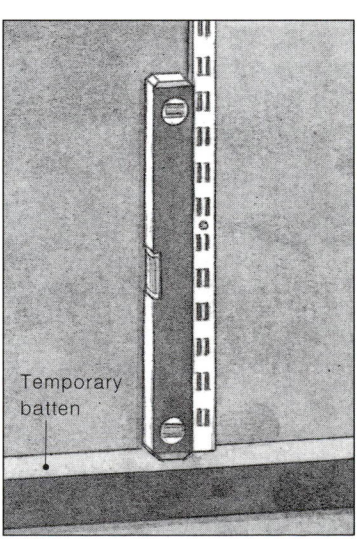
Temporary batten

HOW TO ATTACH ADJUSTABLE SHELVING

When attaching the shelving to a solid wall, measure the wall and decide how many uprights are required. You will need one at each end and intermediate uprights spaced a maximum of 24in (610mm) apart.

Allowing for wider brackets to be attached at the base of each upright to support the worktop adequately, decide how high you need the shelving supports and cut all the adjustable shelving uprights to this length. Using a hacksaw, cut through at a solid part of the uprights between two pairs of slots.

Hold an upright against the wall at one side and decide at what height it should be. Mark the bottom of the upright on the wall and remove it. Use a straight batten and carpenter's level, or a chalked string line, to draw or snap a straight horizontal line at this height.

Tack a straight batten temporarily to the wall with the batten's top edge level with the marked line. Mark along the batten where the uprights will be attached. Use a metal detector to check that there are no electric cables or water pipes in the wall at these points.

Rest one of the slotted uprights on the end batten and, holding a carpenter's level against the upright to ensure that it is vertical, use a pencil to mark the screw fixing points.

Drill the wall at the marked points, insert anchors, and screw the upright in place. Repeat for the other uprights. Make sure that the slots are exactly in line with each other.

Measure the spaces between the uprights and cut the bulletin board panels to fit. Cover them with felt and fit the panels by screwing to the wall, using screw cups under the heads for neatness. For an invisible fixing, glue the panels in place with panel adhesive or hang them using keyhole plates attached to the backs of the panels and hooked over woodscrews inserted in anchors.

Finally, slot the brackets into place, fit the shelves, and screw them to the brackets from the underside.

5 Bulletin Board Panels
Fit bulletin boards by screwing through using screw cups or by hanging on keyhole plates.

6 Screwing Bracket and Shelf
Slot brackets into place and attach shelves to the brackets by screwing through from the underside.

7 Attaching to Hollow Walls
On hollow walls screw three horizontal battens to wall, screwing through into the main wall studs.

8 Installing Plan Brackets
Temporarily attach vertical batten to wall to align brackets. Drill, anchor, and screw them to wall.

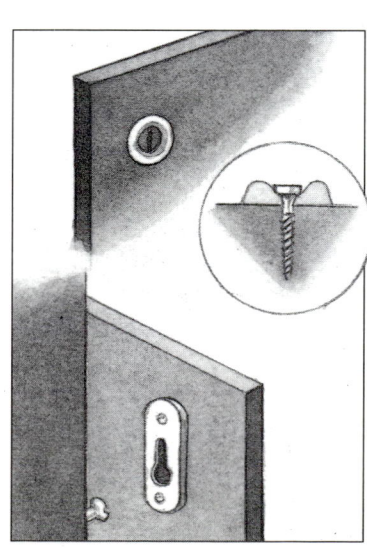

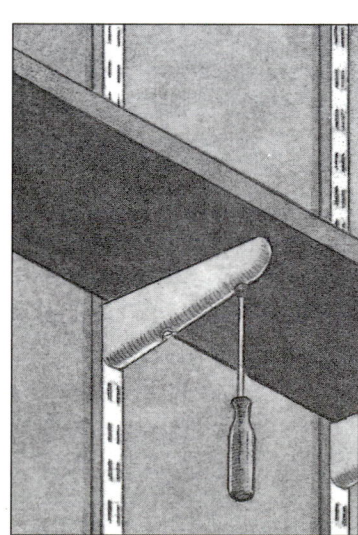

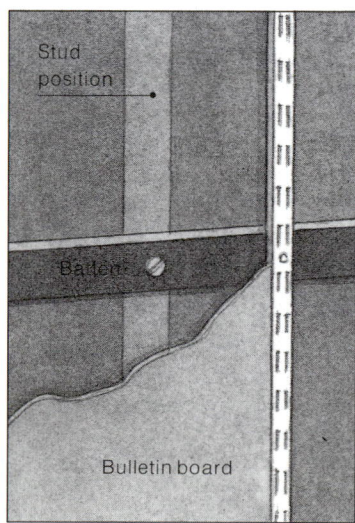

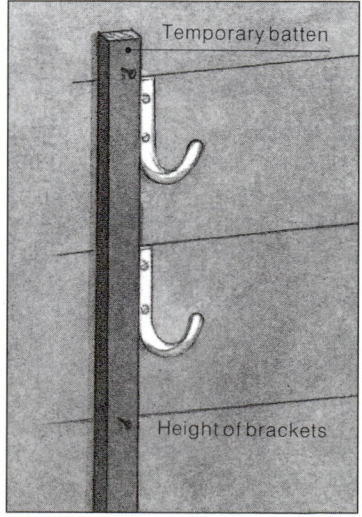

REPLACING BASEBOARDS

It is attention to detail that adds the finishing touch to a room. In this hallway (left) the traditional handrail and balusters of a half-turn staircase have been boxed-in to give a clean line to this previously dominant feature. A staircase feature like this can be made simply by cladding a sawn lumber frame with $\frac{1}{2}$in (12mm) MDF. The nails should be punched flush with the surface, and the MDF then painted.

The basis of the lumber framework should be the newel posts. They are an integral part of the staircase construction and should be retained.

BUYING AND MAKING BASEBOARDS

In the examples shown here, the baseboards provide the elegant finishing touches.

The type of baseboard shown may be available ready-made from a good lumberyard. The size normally available is 1 × 9in (25 × 225mm). Made from softwood, it can be stained with

wood dye if required.

If you cannot find a ready-made baseboard, try a specialist lumberyard, which may have a milling machine capable of producing the exact molding you require.

There are two ways in which to produce an elaborate molding yourself. The easiest is to build one up as shown (fig 2) by combining plain planks with suitable ready-made moldings or beadings. This may not produce exactly what is required, but will provide an acceptable match.

For an exact match you need a router and one or two cutters from a specialist router bit manufacturer. First, draw the outline of the molding on to lined tracing paper. If you are copying a molding, a contour gauge makes this an easy task. By studying the outline you will be able to break it down into its various shapes, which you can match up to router bits from the range available. You can then build up the molding by making several passes with the router, changing router bits and/or the angle of wood as necessary.

① Modernizing a Staircase by Boxing it in
A staircase can be boxed-in by simply nailing sheets of MDF to a lumber frame so that the MDF panels will then appear to be an extension to the surrounding walls.

② Making Baseboard
To match an existing baseboard yourself, build up one with suitable planks and moldings.

③ Attaching to Plastered Wall
Nail the baseboard to wood blocks and a batten which is screwed and anchored to the wall.

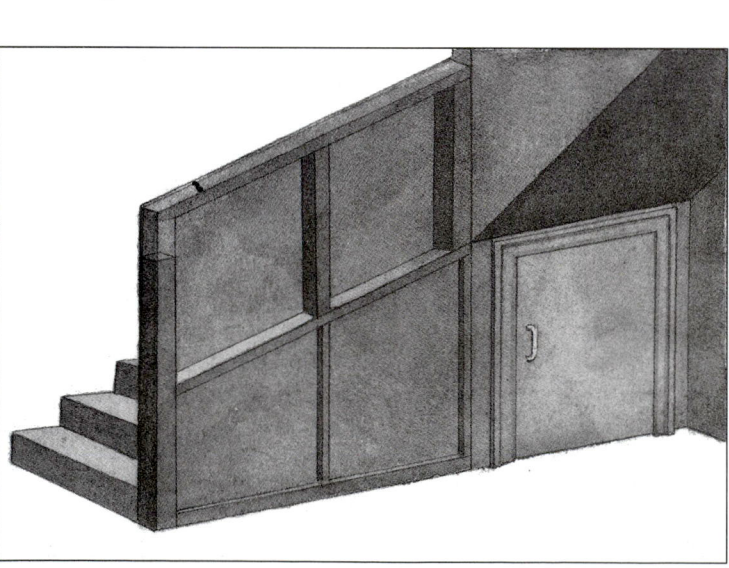

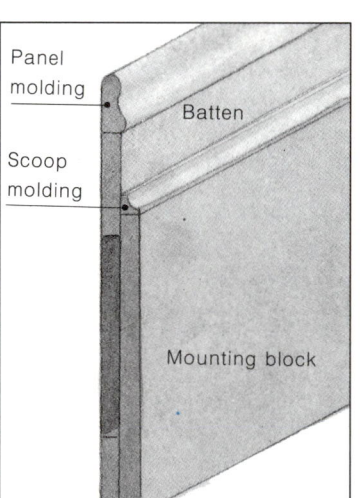

Panel molding
Batten
Scoop molding
Mounting block

GLASS SHELVES

ATTACHING BASEBOARDS AND ARCHITRAVES

When attaching baseboards to a firm, flat base of MDF, the molding can be nailed in place using finishing nails. Punch the nail heads below the surface and fill the indentations, rubbing down the filler before painting.

When attaching a baseboard to a plastered wall, nail it to wood blocks of the same thickness as the plaster layer. The blocks are screwed and anchored to the wall.

At external corners, the edges of the baseboard should be mitered. At internal corners, one baseboard is cut square and is attached to the corner. The end of the adjacent baseboard is scribed to the outline of the first and simply butts against it.

Architraves, the moldings around door frames, are mitered at 45° at the top corners, and at the bottom are cut square with the floor. They are held in place on the surface of the plaster around the door by nailing through them into the door frame.

④ Dealing with Corners
Baseboards and architraves at external corners can be mitered. At internal corners butt join and scribe.

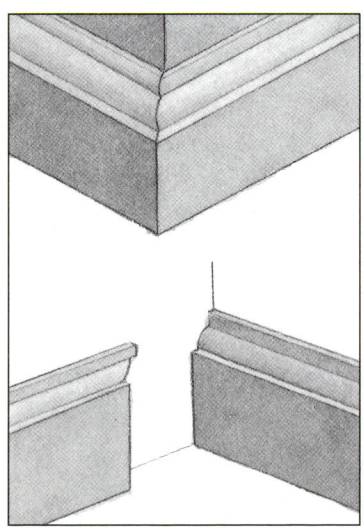

Glass shelves are excellent for display, but the glass must be sufficiently thick to take the load to be placed on it. The supports must be well attached, too.

Ideally, use tempered glass or laminated safety glass, although ordinary float glass can also be used. The important thing is to ensure that the glass is thick enough to carry the load likely to be placed on it, and that the shelf supports are also spaced with this in mind. Ask your glass merchant's advice.

The minimum thickness of glass to be used for shelving is $\frac{1}{4}$in (6mm). This is suitable for light loads only and brackets spaced no further than 16in (400mm) apart. For normal loading, increase the thickness of the glass to $\frac{3}{8}$in (9mm) and the brackets can be spaced up to $27\frac{1}{2}$in (700mm) apart. If the shelves are likely to be heavily loaded – with books, for example – use $\frac{3}{8}$in (9mm) glass, but reduce the bracket spacing to a maximum of $19\frac{1}{2}$in (500mm). For safety, ask the supplier to polish the edges of the glass.

In the photograph here, the glass shelves rest on shelf support studs attached to the side walls of the alcove. There is a wide range of these neat studs in metal and plastic. Sometimes the studs simply screw to the sides of the alcove, but more commonly the studs are pushed into pre-drilled holes, allowing the shelves to be adjustable if a series of holes is drilled. Another way to have adjustable glass shelves is to install a slotted-upright adjustable shelving system for which special glass shelf holding brackets or adaptors are available.

For an "invisible" method of attachment, there are cantilever supports, where a narrow bracket to the full width of the shelf is attached to the rear wall, and the glass shelf is slotted into the bracket.

For bathrooms, there is a wide range of glass shelf support brackets, usually with a chrome finish.

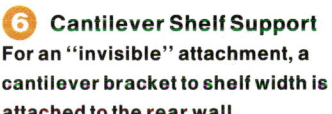

⑤ A Selection of Supports
A selection of support brackets for glass shelves; some for permanent shelves; stud types are adjustable.

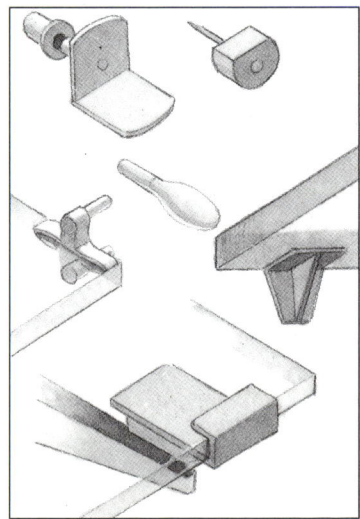

⑥ Cantilever Shelf Support
For an "invisible" attachment, a cantilever bracket to shelf width is attached to the rear wall.

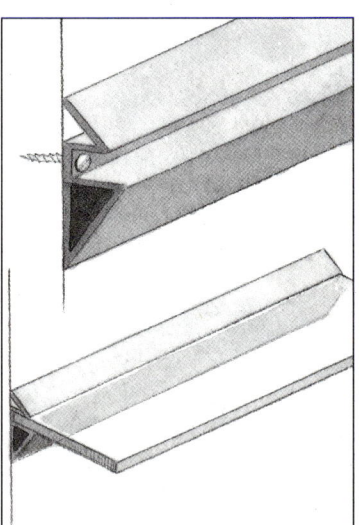

Tools

Adhesive spreader These are palm-size pieces of semi-flexible plastic with serrated or notched edges which are used to spread adhesives over wide surfaces, evenly, and at the correct rate. Because the size of the serrations or notches affects the spreading rate, adhesive manufacturers usually supply a spreader with their adhesives for brands where a spreader is required: mainly contact-types and tiling and flooring adhesives.

Bench stop and vise A woodwork vise is fitted to the underside of a bench, with the jaws level with the bench top. The jaws are lined and topped with hardwood to protect the work and any tools being used. Some vises also incorporate a small steel peg (a "dog") that can be raised above the main jaw level. This allows awkward or long pieces of wood to be clamped in position when used with a bench stop which is fixed at the opposite end of the bench stop.

Sliding bevel (1) Also called a bevel gauge, this is a type of square used to mark out lumber at any required angle. The sliding blade can be locked against the stock by means of a locking lever and the blade can form any angle with the stock.

Marking gauge (2) Essential for setting out woodworking joints, this is used to mark both widths and thicknesses with only a light scratch. The gauge comprises a handle, on which slides a stock bearing a steel marking pin. This movable stock can be locked in any position with a thumb screw so the steel pin is fixed at a precise point.

Mortise gauge (3) Similar to a marking gauge, it has two pins – one fixed, one adjustable – to mark out both sides of a mortise at the same time. Some types have an additional pin fixed below the beam so that the tool can be used as a marking gauge.

Contour gauge This is also called a shape tracer or a scribing gauge. It comprises a row of steel pins or plastic fingers held in a central bar. When pressed against an object, like a baseboard, the pins follow the shape of the object.

Utility knife A razor-sharp blade which is used to score a thin, accurate line for a saw or chisel to follow, ensuring a precise cut. The flat face of the knife can be run against the blade of a try square or straight-edge. A paring chisel is placed in the knife line for accurate paring of the last cut.

Miter box A simple open-topped wooden box which is used to guide saws into material at a fixed 45° or 90° angle, to ensure a square cut.

Plumb bob and chalk A plumb line is used to check verticals and mark accurate vertical lines, in chalk, on walls. A plumb bob is simply a pointed weight attached to a long length of string. Before use, the string can be rubbed with a stick of colored chalk. Hold the string in the required position at the top, wait for the plumb bob to stop swinging, then carefully press the string against the wall at the bottom and then pluck the string to leave a line on the wall. Most hardware stores stock chalk lines (plumb bobs with line winders and powdered chalk containers): these save time by automatically dusting the line with chalk as it is withdrawn.

Portable workbench A collapsible, portable workbench is vital for woodworking. A large, fixed workbench in a garage or shed is important, but the major advantage of the portable type is that it is lightweight and can be carried to the job, where it provides sturdy support when final adjustments have to be made.

A portable bench is like a giant vise – the worksurface comprises two sections which can be opened wide or closed tightly according to the dimensions of the work and the nature of the task. It can hold large and awkward objects.

Scribing block To fit an item neatly against a wall (which is very unlikely to be perfectly flat) the item has to be "scribed" flat to the wall using a small block of wood and a pencil (see **Techniques, page 91**). A scribing block is simply an offcut of wood measuring about 1in × 1in × 1in (25mm × 25mm × 25mm). The block is held against the wall, a sharp pencil is held against the opposite end of the block, and the block and the pencil are moved in a unit along the wall to mark a line on the item to be fitted. If you cut to this line, the item will then fit tightly against the wall.

Carpenter's level (9) Used for checking that surfaces are horizontal or vertical. A 24in (610mm) long level is the most useful all-round size. An aluminum or steel level will withstand knocks and it can be either I-girder or box-shaped in section. Ideally, a 9in (225mm) "torpedo" carpenter's level is also useful to have, for working in confined spaces such as alcoves and inside cupboards. It may be used in conjunction with a straight-edge over longer surfaces.

Steel measuring tape A 12ft (3.6m) or 18ft (5.5m) long, lockable tape (metal or plastic) is best, and one with a window in the casing that makes it easier to read measurements.

Steel bench rule Since the rule is made of steel, the graduations are very precise and indelible. A rule graduated on both sides in imperial and metric is the most useful. The rule can also serve as a precise straight-edge for marking cutting lines.

Straight-edge Can be made from a piece of 1 × 2in (25 × 50mm) scrap wood. It is used to tell whether a surface is flat and also for checking whether two points are aligned with each other.

Try square (4) An L-shaped precision tool comprising a steel blade and stock (or handle) set at a perfect right angle to each other on both

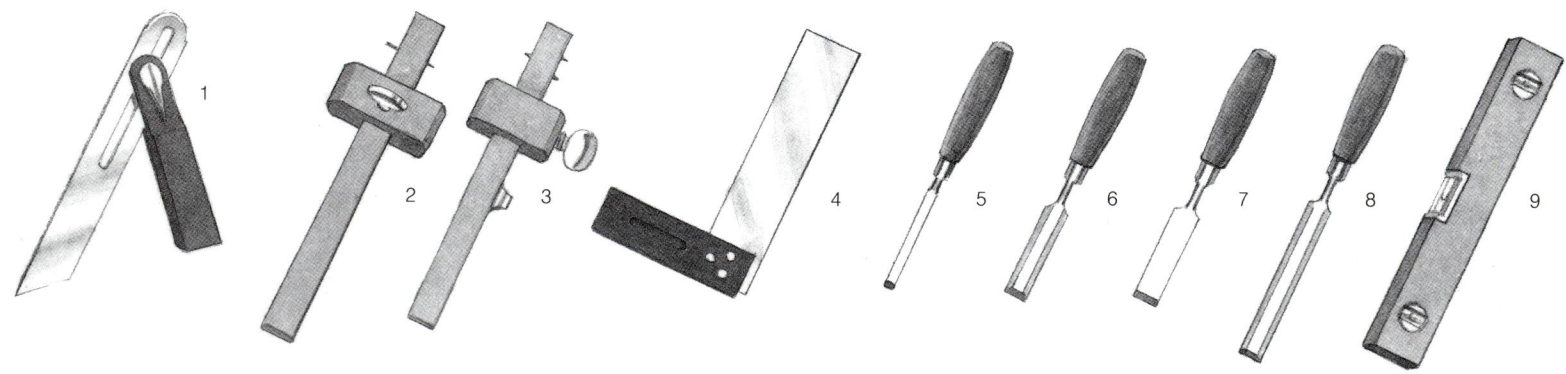

TOOLS, MATERIALS, AND TECHNIQUES

Tools for Sharpening and Cutting

72/73

the inside and outside edges. Used for marking cutting lines at right angles to an edge and for checking a square.

SUPPLEMENTARY TOOLS

Drill stand Enables a power drill to be used with extreme accuracy when, for example, joining doweling (*see* **Techniques, page 90**). The hole will be perpendicular to the surface and its depth can be carefully controlled. The drill is lowered on to the work with a spring-loaded lever which gives good control and accuracy.

Metal detector Pinpoints metal objects such as electric cables and water and gas pipes hidden in walls, ceilings, and floors. Electronically operated, it buzzes or flashes when metal is found.

TOOLS FOR SHARPENING AND CUTTING

Chisels Used to cut slots in wood or to pare off thin slivers. Some chisels may be used with a mallet when cutting slots. When new, a chisel's cutting edge is ground and must be honed with an oilstone to sharpen it.
Mortise chisel (5) Used with a mallet for cutting deep slots.
Bench chisel (6) Used for undercutting in confined spaces, such as when making dovetail joints.
Firmer chisel (7) For general-purpose use around the home.
Paring chisel (8) Has a long blade for cutting deep joints or long grooves.

Doweling jig A simple doweling jig clamps on to a piece of work, ensuring that the drill is aligned accurately over the center of the dowel hole to be drilled. It also guides the drill vertically.

DRILLS

Hand drill (10) For drilling holes for screws or for making large holes, particularly in wood. It will

make holes in metal and is useful where there is no power source. A handle attached to a toothed wheel is used to turn the drill in its chuck.
Power drill (11) These range from a simple, single-speed model (which will drill holes only in soft materials) to a multi-speed drill with electronic control. Most jobs call for something in between the two, such as a two-speed drill with hammer action. The two speeds enable most hard materials to be drilled and the hammer action means that you can also drill into the hardest walls.

DRILL BITS

You will need a selection of twist bits in various sizes and of different types for wood and metal, for use with a drill.

Brad-point bit (12) Used to make dowel holes in wood. The tip has two cutting spurs on the side and a center point to prevent the bit from wandering off center. Diameters range from $\frac{1}{8}$in (3mm) to $\frac{1}{2}$in (12mm).
Twist drill bit (13) Used with an electric drill for drilling small holes in wood and metal. Carbon-steel drills are for wood only: drilling into metal requires a high-speed steel drill.
Masonry bit (14) Has a specially hardened tungsten-carbide tip for drilling into masonry to the exact size required for an anchor. Special percussion drill bits are available for use with a hammer drill when boring into concrete.
Countersink bit (15) After a hole is drilled in wood, a countersink bit is used to cut a recess for the screwhead to sit in, so ensuring that it lies below the surface. Different types are available for use with a carpenter's brace and an electric drill. Head diameters are $\frac{3}{8}$in (9mm), $\frac{1}{2}$in (12mm), and $\frac{9}{16}$in (15mm). Carbon-steel bits can be used for wood, but high-speed steel bits can be used for wood, plastic, or metal.
Spade bit (16) Is used with an electric drill. It has a point at the end of the shank and its flat shank end allows it to slot into the drill chuck. Diameters are from $\frac{1}{4}$in (6mm) to $1\frac{1}{2}$in (38mm). For maxi-

mum efficiency the bit must be turned at high speed from about 1000 to 2000 rpm. It can be used to drill into cross grain, end grain, and manmade boards. Also known as a speedbore bit.
Auger bit (17) Has a tapered, square shank that fits into a carpenter's brace. It is used to make deep holes in wood, the usual lengths being up to 10in (250mm). Diameters range from $\frac{1}{4}$in (6mm) to $1\frac{1}{2}$in (38mm). The tip has a screw thread to draw the bit into the wood.
Forstner bit (18) A Forstner bit, or hinge-sinker bit, is primarily used for boring $1\frac{3}{8}$in (35mm) or 1in (25mm) diameter flat bottomed holes in cabinet and wardrobe doors to accept the hinge bosses on concealed hinges. Forstner bits are used in electric drills, ideally fitted in drill stands, and set to drill no deeper than $\frac{1}{2}$in (12mm).

Oilstone and honing guide The first sharpens and the second maintains the correct angle for sharpening chisel and plane blades. An oilstone is a rectangular block of stone with grit on both sides. Oil is used as a lubricant while the blade is being sharpened on the stone, so you will need a can of fine oil nearby.
 The honing guide is an inexpensive tool which makes sharpening easier and more efficient. The blade of the tool to be sharpened is inserted at an angle and clamped in place, then the guide is repeatedly rolled back and forth on the surface of the oilstone.

Power router (19) This portable electric tool is used to cut grooves, recesses, and many types of joints in lumber, as well as to shape the edges of long lumber battens to form decorative moldings. A whole range of cutting bits in different shapes and sizes is available and when fitted into the router the bits revolve at very high speed (about 25,000 rpm) to cut the wood smoothly and cleanly (20). Although hand routers (which look like small planes) are available, whenever routers are referred to in this book, it is the power router to which the remarks are directed.

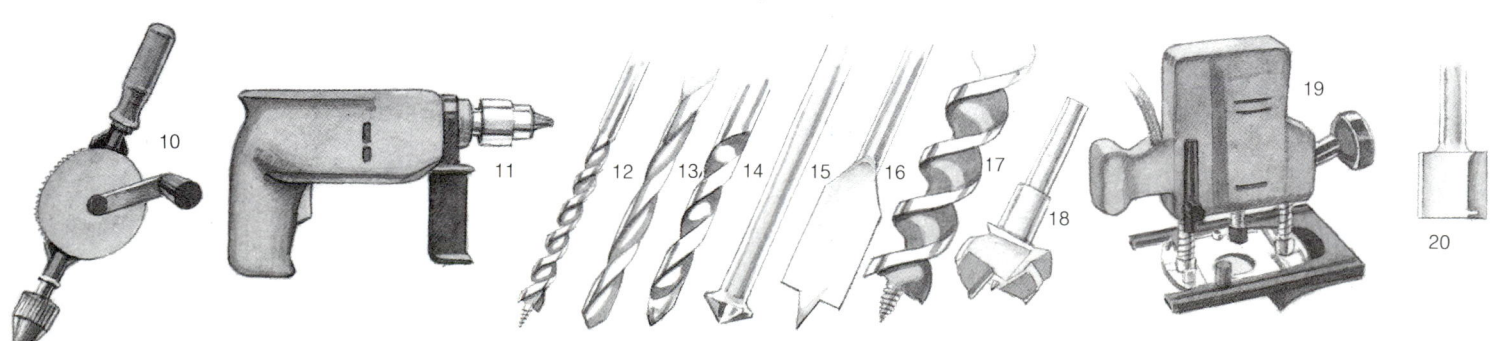

TOOLS

SAWS

Circular saw (1) Invaluable for cutting large pieces of lumber or sheets of board. It will also cut grooves and angles. The most popular size has a diameter of $7\frac{1}{4}$in (184mm). Circular saws can be extremely dangerous and must be used carefully. The piece of work must be held securely and the blade depth set so that it will not cut into anything below the work. The tool should be fitted with an upper and lower blade guard. Support your work on scrap battens to avoid cutting into work-benches or floors.

Coping saw (2) Used to make curved or circular cuts. It has a narrow blade, which can be swiveled. When cutting, the blade can be angled as necessary so that the frame clears the edge of the work. Drill a hole close to the edge of the piece to be cut out, and thread the coping saw blade through the hole before reconnecting it to the handle and starting to cut.

Dovetail saw (3) Also called a gent's saw. This fine-tooth form of back saw with a stiffened back is ideal for making delicate and precise saw cuts. It is particularly useful for making dovetail joints.

Hand saws (4) Are used for rough cutting rather than fine carpentry. They have a flexible blade of 20–26in (510–670mm) in length, and a wooden or plastic handle. They are useful for general-purpose cutting of wood and fiberboards.

Saber saw (7) Will cut a variety of materials, and is much more versatile than a circular saw, although not as quick or powerful. It also cuts curves, shapes, angles, and holes in the middle of panels. The best models offer variable speeds – slow for hard materials and fast for soft. The latest models have either a reciprocating or a pendulum action. In these cases the blade goes backwards and forwards as well as up and down, which allows for much faster cutting on straight lines.

Compass saw (5) Also called a keyhole saw, it is designed to cut holes and shapes in wood. It has a narrow, tapered blade which will cut keyholes, for example. A hole is first drilled and the saw blade inserted to make the cut. Compass saws are useful for cutting holes for inset sinks where a power Saber saw is not available.

Back saw (6) For cutting the tenon part of a mortise and tenon joint (*see* **Techniques, page 88**), and also useful for other delicate and accurate work. It has a stiffened back and the blade is about 10–12in (250–300mm) long.

Surforms Available in a range of lengths from approximately 6–10in (150–250mm), these rasps are useful for the initial shaping of wood. However, further fine finishing by hand is needed to obtain a smooth surface. The steel blade has a pattern of alternating small teeth and holes through which waste wood passes, so that the teeth do not get clogged up. When blunt, the blade is simply replaced.

SUPPLEMENTARY TOOLS

Hacksaw For cutting metal. A traditional hacksaw has a wooden handle and a solid metal frame. The blade is tensioned by a wing-nut. Modern hacksaws have a tubular frame which is adjustable for different lengths of blade. A "junior" hacksaw is ideal for sawing small items or for working in confined spaces.

HANDS TOOLS

Awl Used to make a small pilot hole in wood to take a screw. It is twisted into the wood with a continuous circular movement.

CLAMPS

For securing glued pieces of work while they are setting. There are many types of clamp, but the C-clamp is the most commonly used and is available in a wide range of jaw sizes.

Folding wedges are sometimes useful for securing an object while it is being glued. You can make two by cutting diagonally through a block of wood. For instructions on how to make and use folding wedges, see page 81.

Bar clamps These employ a long metal bar, and are indispensable for holding together large frameworks. Initially, rent rather than buy bar clamps, although you can improvise in some cases by making a rope tourniquet. This consists of a piece of rope which is tied around the object and a length of stick to twist the rope and so clamp the frame tightly.

Band clamp A nylon webbing clamp to apply even pressure around frames when they are being assembled. The webbing, like narrow seat-belt type material, is looped around the frame, pulled as tight as possible by hand, and then finally tightened by means of a screw mechanism or ratchet winder. Band clamps are cheaper alternatives to bar clamps.

C-clamp Also called a frame clamp or fast-action clamp, it is important for our projects that the jaws of the clamp open at least 8in (200mm). The lumber to be held in the clamp is placed between the jaws which are then tightened by turning a thumb-screw, tommy bar, or other type of handle. In the case of the fast-action clamp, one jaw is free to slide on a bar, and after sliding this jaw up to the workpiece, final tightening is achieved by turning the handle. In all cases, to prevent damage to the workpiece, scraps of wood are placed between it and the jaws of the clamp.

HAMMERS

Claw hammer (9) The claw side of the head of the hammer is used to extract nails from a piece of work quickly and cleanly.

Cross-peen hammer (10) The peen is the tapered section opposite the flat hammer head, and it is used for starting off small brads and tacks held in the fingers.

Tack hammer A smaller version of the cross-peen, this is useful for light work.

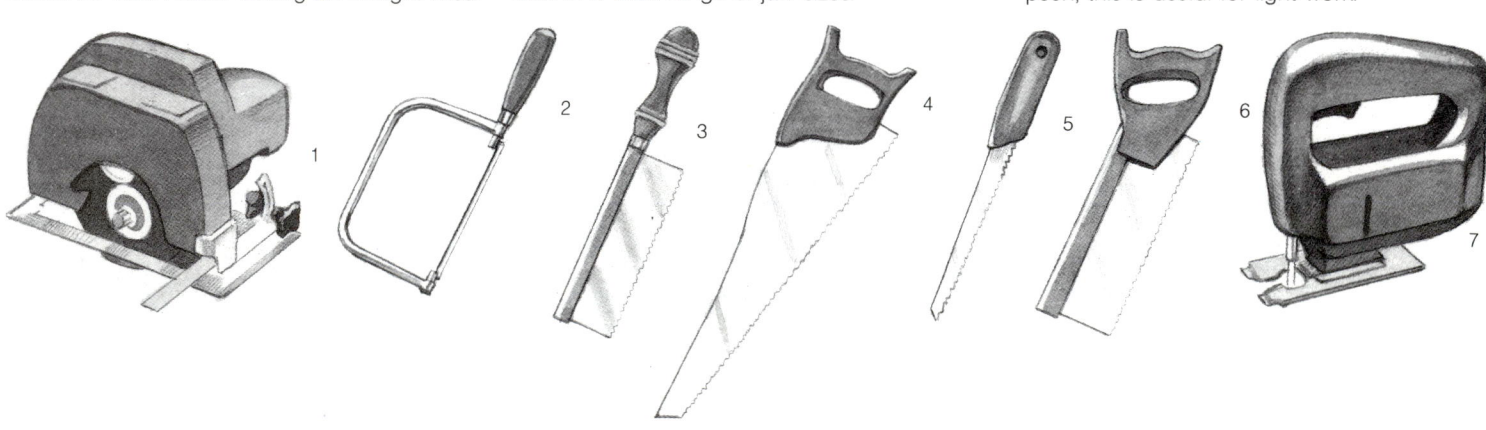

Mallet Most commonly used to strike mortise chisels, although if a chisel has an impact-resistant handle then a hammer may also be used. The tapered wooden head ensures square contact with the object being struck.

Nailset Used with a hammer to drive nails and brads below the surface so that they are hidden; the hole can then be filled. The pointed end is "cupped" to fit neatly over a nail or brad head.

Orbital sander Otherwise known as a finishing sander, this gives a fine, smooth surface finish to wood. A gritted sanding sheet is fitted to the sander's base plate. Sheets are graded from coarse to fine, and the grade used depends on the roughness of the surface to be sanded. Orbital sanders produce a great deal of dust, so always wear a mask when using one.

Pliers Used to remove nails and tacks from wood. The bevel-edged jaws grip the nail close to the surface of the wood, and the pliers are rocked back and forth to extract it.

PLANES

Smoothing plane (11) A general-purpose, hand-held plane for smoothing and straightening surfaces and edges. The plane is about 10in (250mm) long and its blade 2–2¼in (50–60mm) wide. The wider the blade the better the finish on wide lumber. There is a fine adjustment for depth of cut and a lever for lateral adjustment.

Block plane (12) Held in the palm of the hand, it is easy to use for small work and beveling edges. Also useful for planing end grain.

Jack plane (13) Longer than a smoothing plane, it is used for straightening long edges and is a good all-purpose plane.

Power plane (14) Finishes lumber to precise dimensions. A one-hand model is lightweight and can be used anywhere, whereas the heavier two-hander is intended for workbench use. A power plane will also cut bevels and rabbets.

Rasp A rasp is a type of coarse file for wood, available with flat or half-round surfaces. It is used to shape wood, often when scribing an edge to fit against a wall.

Sanding block and sanding paper A sanding block is used with sanding paper to finish and smooth flat surfaces. The block is made of cork, rubber, or softwood and the sanding paper is wrapped around it. Make sure in doing so that the paper is not wrinkled. Sanding paper used without a block tends to produce an uneven surface. Sheets of sanding paper are graded from coarse to fine and are selected according to the roughness of the surface to be sanded. Coarse paper is used for a very rough surface and fine paper for finishing.

Screwdrivers There is no single type of screwdriver that is better than the rest; personal preference is what matters. They come in many shapes and sizes, and the main differences are the type of tip (for slotted or Phillips screws), the length, and the shape of the handle, which varies from straight or fluted to bulb-shaped. Phillips screwdrivers can be used on most Phillips screws but certain speciality recess screws require their own special screwdrivers.

Ideally, you should have a range of screwdrivers for dealing with all sizes of screws. Ratchet models, which return the handle to its starting point, are easy to operate since your hand grip does not need to change. The spiral action screwdriver is very efficient (though very expensive) and it works like a bicycle pump rather than by turning the handle.

Cordless screwdriver A fairly new tool, it is expensive but can save much time and effort. Mainly used for Phillips screws.

SUPPLEMENTARY TOOLS

Metal file Gives a metal edge the required shape and finish. Most files are supplied with a removable handle which can be transferred to a

file of a different size. A flat or half-round file (one side flat, the other curved) are good general-purpose tools.

Hand staple gun A trigger-operated tool which fires a staple straight into a surface, usually fabric, fiberboard, or thin wood over a wooden batten. Its advantage over conventional nailing with a hammer is that, as it is used one-handed, the other hand is free to hold the work.

Power staple gun Easier to fire. Fires heavy-duty staples into thicker surfaces, such as ceilings. It is preferable to buy the same brand of gun and staples to prevent jamming.

Paintbrushes A set of paintbrushes for painting and varnishing should ideally comprise three sizes – 1in (25mm), 2in (50mm), and 3in (75mm). A better finish is always achieved by matching the size of brush to the surface – a small brush for narrow surfaces, a large brush for wide areas. Always clean thoroughly after use.

Electric paint sprayer Can produce a very smooth finish once its use is mastered. It may be preferable to hire rather than buy one – initially at least – since airless spray guns and compressors are expensive. Always work parallel to the surface you are spraying, applying two thin coats of paint rather than one thick coat.

Wrench A wrench is required for tightening carriage bolts, and any type that fits the head of the bolt is suitable. If the correct-size open-ended or ring wrench is not available, any type of adjustable wrench may be used.

Caulking gun Used to eject a bead of mastic-type waterproofing sealants (or caulking) into gaps where water might penetrate, such as around shower trays. A cartridge of caulking or sealant is held in the frame (or "gun"), and a plunger, pushes the caulking out of a nozzle at the end of the cartridge.

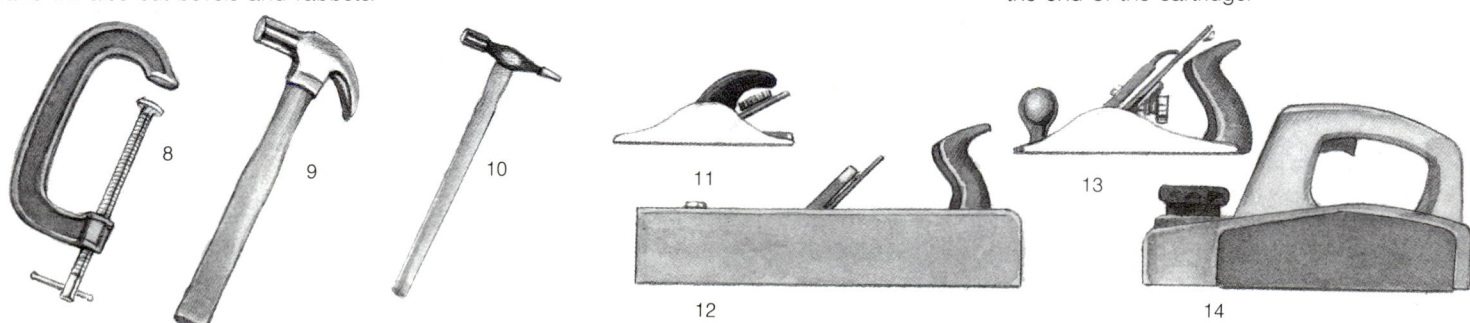

MATERIALS

LUMBER

Lumber is classified into two groups – softwoods and hardwoods. Softwoods come from evergreen trees and hardwoods from deciduous trees. Check lumber for defects before buying it. Avoid wood which is badly cracked or split, although you need not be concerned about fine, surface cracks since these can be planed, sanded, or filled. Do not buy warped wood, as it will be impossible to work with. Check for warping by looking along the length of a board to see if there is any bowing or twisting.

When you get your wood home, condition it for about ten days. As the wood will have been stored in the open air at the yard, it will be "wet." Once indoors, it dries, shrinks slightly and will warp unless stored flat on the ground. If you build with wood as soon as you get it home, your structure could run into problems later as the wood dries out. To avoid warping and aid drying, stack boards in a pile, with offcuts of wood placed between each board to allow air to circulate. This will lower the moisture content to about 10% and condition the wood, ready for use.

Softwood Softwood is much less expensive than hardwood and is used in general building work. Softwood is sold either by the *lineal* foot or the *board* foot. The former is based on the length of a piece of wood – for example, 8ft of 1 by 2 (1 × 2in [25 × 50mm]). The board foot is calculated by the thickness in inches × width in feet × length in feet – for example, 10ft of 1 by 6 would be 5 board feet: 1in × $\frac{1}{2}$ft (6in) × 10ft.

It is important to remember that standard softwood sizes refer to sawn sizes – that is, how it is sawn at a mill. When bought this way, softwood is suitable only for rough constructional work such as floor joists and basic frames. However, the smooth wood used for the projects in this book, for which appearance and accuracy are important, will need to have been planed. This is the state in which softwood is commonly sold in

local lumberyards; in the trade it is referred to as "S4S" (smooth 4 sides), and, since planing takes a little off each face, planed softwood is $\frac{1}{4}$–$\frac{3}{4}$in (6–9mm) smaller in width and thickness than its stated size. Standard sizes should, therefore, be thought of as rough guides rather than exact measurements.

Hardwood Expensive and not as easy to obtain as softwoods, hardwoods often have to be ordered or bought from a specialist lumberyard. Many lumberyards will machine-plane lumber to your exact specifications. In home woodwork, hardwood is usually confined to moldings and beadings, which are used to give exposed sawn edges a neat finish.

SHEET MATERIAL BOARDS

Sheet material boards are mechanically made from wood and other fibers. They are versatile, relatively inexpensive, made to uniform quality, and are available in large sheets. Sheet materials are graded according to the quality of finished surfaces. It is worth buying the best you can afford, bearing in mind the purpose for which you will be using it. You need to know the advantages of each type of board before making your choice. All boards are made in sheets of 4 × 8ft (1220 × 2440mm), and most stockists will saw them to the size you require.

Hardboard Also called masonite, and the best known fiberboard. Common thicknesses are $\frac{1}{8}$in, $\frac{3}{16}$in, and $\frac{1}{4}$in (3mm, 4mm, and 6mm). As hardboard is weak and has to be supported on a framework, it is essentially a material for paneling. Denser types of tempered hardboard can be used for cladding partitions; softer types for bulletin boards.

Medium board Softer and weaker than hardboard, it is often, therefore, used in thicker sheets – usually $\frac{1}{2}$in (12mm).

Medium-density fiberboard (MDF) A good, highly compressed, general-purpose building board. You may find that it has to be ordered from a plywood wholesaler (your retail yard can do this for you), but it is worth it since it does not flake or splinter when cut, and leaves a clean, hard-sawn edge which does not need to be disguised as do other fiberboards. It also takes a very good paint finish, even on its edges. Thicknesses range from around $\frac{3}{16}$in to 1$\frac{3}{8}$in (5mm to 35mm).

Particleboard Made by binding wood chips together under pressure, it is rigid, dense, and fairly heavy. Particleboard is strong when reasonably well supported, but sawing it can leave an unstable edge and can also quickly blunt a saw. Ordinary screws do not hold well in particleboard, and it is best to use twin-threaded screws (*see* **Screws, page 78**). Most grades of particleboard are not moisture-resistant and will swell up when wet. Thicknesses range from $\frac{1}{4}$–1$\frac{1}{2}$in (6–40mm), but $\frac{1}{2}$in, $\frac{3}{4}$in, and 1in (12mm, 19mm, and 25mm) are the most common.

Particleboard is widely available with the faces and edges veneered with natural wood, PVC, or plastic laminates. Colored finishes and imitation wood-grain effects are also available.

If used for shelving, particleboard must be well supported on closely-spaced brackets or bearers. The better-quality laminated boards are far stronger than plain particleboard.

Plywood Made by gluing thin wood veneers together in plies (layers) with the grain in each ply running at right angles to that of its neighbors. This gives the board strength and helps prevent warping. The most common boards have three, five, or seven plies. Plywood is graded for quality, taking into account the amount of knots and surface markings present: N is perfect but often has to be ordered, followed by A, B, C, and D in decreasing order of quality; D is for rough work only. For example, A2 means that both faces are of very good quality; AC or ACX (the "X" stands

MOLDINGS (see page 78)

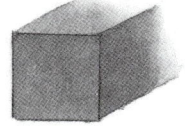

Square

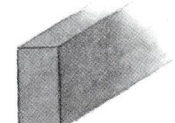

Rectangular

Scoop

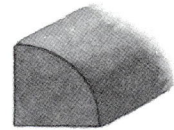

Quarter round

Corner

for exterior) denotes A grade on one side and C on the other, and is a good, economical option where only one side will be visible.

MR (moisture-resistant) plywood is for *internal* jobs where damp conditions prevail. Plywood is available with a range of surface veneers such as teak or mahogany, or with a plastic finish. Common thicknesses are $\frac{1}{8}$in, $\frac{1}{4}$in, $\frac{1}{2}$in, and $\frac{3}{4}$in (3mm, 6mm, 12mm, and 19mm).

Lumber core Made by sandwiching natural lumber strips between wood veneers, the latter usually of Far Eastern redwood or plain birch. Although plain birch is a little more expensive than redwood, it is of a much better quality. Lumber core is very strong, but can leave an ugly edge when sawn (gaps often appear between the core strips), making edge fixings difficult. It is graded in the same way as plywood and common thicknesses are $\frac{1}{2}$in, $\frac{3}{4}$in, and 1in (12mm, 19mm, and 25mm). It is a very rigid board and is therefore ideal for a long span of shelving.

Tongued-and-grooved boards Also called match boarding, or matching, this is widely used for cladding frameworks and walls. Each board has a tongue on one side and a slot on the other side. The tongue fits into the slot on the adjacent board to form an area of cladding; this expands and contracts according to temperature and humidity without cracks opening up between boards.

Ordinary tongued-and-grooved boards fit together like floorboards, but tongued and grooved boards for cladding have some form of decoration; this can be a beaded joint, or, more commonly, beveled edge which forms the attractive V-joint of tongued, grooved, and V-jointed (TGV) boards.

ADHESIVES AND FILLERS

Adhesives Modern types are strong and efficient. If they fail, it is because the wrong adhesive

is being used or the manufacturer's instructions are not followed carefully. For all general indoor woodworking, use an aliphatic resin (yellow woodworker's glue) – all glue manufacturers produce their own brands. Use a two part resorcinol glue (guaranteed waterproof) in areas where there may be water splashing or condensation. If joints do not meet perfectly, use a gap-filling adhesive.

Ceramic tiles require their own special adhesive (of a thick, buttery consistency) which is supplied, ready mixed, in tubs. If tiles are likely to be regularly splashed – around sinks for example – you should use a waterproof tile adhesive. Some brands of adhesive can also double as grouting cement for filling the gaps between tiles.

Fillers If the wood is to be painted over, use a standard plastic wood filler – the type for repairing cracks in walls. This dries white and will be evident if used under any other kind of finish. When a clear finish is needed, fill cracks and holes with a proprietary wood filler or stopping. These are thick pastes and come in a range of wood colors. You can mix them together or add a wood stain if the color you want is not available. It is best to choose a color slightly paler than the surrounding wood, since fillers tend to darken when the finish is applied. Test the filler first on a waste piece of matching wood.

In fine work, a grain-filler is used to stop the final finish sinking into the wood. This is a paste, thinned with white spirit, and then rubbed into the surface. It is supplied in a range of wood shades.

FINISHES

The choice of finish is determined by whether the wood or board will be hidden, painted, or enhanced by a protective clear finish.

LACQUER

Quick-drying cellulose lacquer is the best finishing treatment to apply to wood furniture. It is resistant

to heat, scratches, and solvents, and, when sprayed on, produces a superb finish.

POLISHES

French polish Refers to a particular polish, but it is also the collective term for all polishes made with shellac and alcohol. French polish is ideal where a light to medium brown tone is required. Although it gives a fine reflection, the finish itself is not highly protective.

Button polish Will give a more golden or orange tone.

White French polish or **transparent polish** Produces a clear finish, allowing the natural color of the wood to show through. French polishing demands great skill, and many people prefer to apply a clear polyurethane varnish with a conventional wax polish covering it.

PAINT

A liquid gloss (oil-based) paint is suitable for wood, and is applied after a suitable undercoat. Generally, two thin coats of gloss are better than one thick coat. Non-drip gloss paint is an alternative. It has a jelly-like consistency and does not require an undercoat, although a quality finish may need a second coat. Use a liquid gloss if you want to spray paint.

VARNISH

Normally applied by brush, varnish can also be sprayed on. It is available as a gloss, satin, or matt finish, all clear. However, varnish also comes in a range of colors, so that you can change the color of the wood and protect it simultaneously. The color does not sink into the wood, so that if the surface becomes scratched or marked then its original color will show through. For this reason, a wood stain or dye is sometimes used to change the color of wood. It sinks into the wood, but offers no protection, so a varnish or clear lacquer will also be needed.

Half round

Twice rounded

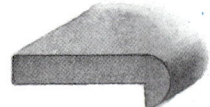

Hockey stick

Reeded

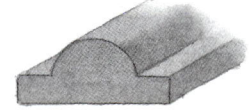

Astragal

Moldings, Battens, and Dowels

Moldings   Wood moldings are used as ornamentation and to cover gaps or fixtures in a wooden construction. The term "molding" encompasses everything from a simple, thin edge-banding to architraves and baseboards. A variety of shaped cutters produce many different shapes and sizes. In the unlikely event of your being unable to buy the shape of molding you want, you could make your own using a router.

Moldings are cut from hardwood – usually poplar or basswood. You can buy more exotic hardwood moldings, mahogany for example, from a specialist lumberyard. These are expensive and you may well prefer to buy a cheaper molding and then to stain or varnish it to obtain the color that you want.

Decorative moldings are available in standard lengths of 6ft, 8ft, 10ft, and 12ft. The following types are among those which are ideal for edging manmade boards and are available in a variety of sizes: half round (or bullnose); twice rounded; hockey stick; reeded; and astragal. Square or rectangular moldings range from $\frac{1}{4} \times \frac{1}{4}$in (6×6mm) up to $\frac{1}{4} \times 1$in (6×25mm).

Other types of molding include scoop and quarter round, which cover gaps between the meeting parts of a structure. Corner moldings are a plain version of the scoop, and can be used inside or outside a joint.

When buying moldings, check each one to make sure that the length is straight and free from large or dead knots, which are likely to fall out and leave holes. Fungal staining is something else to watch for, especially if you intend to use a clear finish. If you need several lengths of moldings for the same job, check that you get a good match. Have a close look at the edges, color, and grain of each length, since mismatching can leave surface ripples or uneven edges.

Battens   A general term used to describe a narrow strip of wood. The usual sizes are 1×1in (25×25mm) or 1×2in (25×50mm).

Battens serve one of two main functions. They can be screwed to a wall to serve as bearers for shelves. Alternatively, they can be fixed in a framework on a wall, with sheet material or boards mounted over them to form a new "wall."

Dowels   Used to make framework joints or to join boards edge-to-edge or edge-to-face.

Hardwood dowels are sold in diameters of $\frac{1}{4}$in, $\frac{3}{8}$in, and $\frac{1}{2}$in (6mm, 9mm, and 12mm). You can buy packs of dowels cut to length (either 1in or $1\frac{1}{2}$in [25mm or 38mm]), or you can buy long lengths and cut them to size. Generally speaking, dowel lengths should be about one-and-a-half times the thickness of the boards being joined.

Dowels are used in conjunction with adhesive and, when the joint is complete, it is important to let excess adhesive escape from the joint. Dowels with fluted (finely grooved) sides and beveled ends will help this process. If you have plain rather than shaped dowels, make fine sawcuts along the length and bevel the ends yourself.

Nails

Nails are generally sold by their penny (or "d") size. The most common are 2d (1in), 4d ($1\frac{1}{2}$in), 6d (2in), 8d ($2\frac{1}{2}$in), and 10d (3in).

Common nails   With large, flat, circular heads, these are used for strong joints where frames will be covered, and the nails will be hidden.

Annular threaded nails   Used where really strong attachments are required.

Round finishing nails   Used when the finished appearance is important. The heads of these nails are driven flush with the wood's surface or countersunk so they are unobtrusive. They are also used when nailing a thin piece of wood to a thicker piece and there is a risk of splitting the wood. This is likely when nailing close to the end of the wood, or if the nail is too large.

Brads   For attaching thin panels, these fine, round wire nails will be required. These have tiny, unobtrusive heads that can be driven in flush with the wood's surface or punched below it.

Hardboard pins   Copper-plated and with a square cross-section. They have deep-drive diamond-shaped heads that sink into the surface – ideal for securing hardboard and other boards to lumber in areas subject to condensation, where steel pins could cause black staining.

Masonry nails   For securing lumber battens to walls as an alternative to screwing and anchoring. Where a quick and permanent attachment is required, use the hardened-steel type.

Screws

All types of screws are available with either conventional slotted heads or with Phillips heads. The latter look neater and are the better type to use, especially if you are inserting screws with an electric screwdriver.

For most purposes, screws with flat heads are ideal as, when countersunk, the head lies flush with the surface after insertion. Round-head screws are used for attaching metal fixtures such as shelf brackets and door bolts, which have punched-out rather than countersunk screw holes. Ovalhead screws are often used alone or with metal screw cups where a neat appearance is important.

Wood screws   These have a length of smooth shank just below the head. When joining two pieces of wood, this produces a strong clamping effect as the screw is tightened, but there is also a possibility of the unthreaded shank splitting the wood, so extra care is required.

Twin-threaded screws   Quicker to insert than ordinary wood screws and less likely to split wood. Except for larger sizes, they are threaded along

Nails and Screws

1 Screw cup; 2 Wall anchor bolt; 3 and 4 Frame fixing (nylon plug and plated screw); 5 Veneer pin; 6 Hardboard pin; 7 Brad; 8 Round finishing nail; 9 Common nail; 10 Annular threaded nail; 11 Masonry nail; 12 Countersunk screw with slotted head; 13 Countersunk screw with Phillips head; 14 Round-head screw; 15 Ovalhead screw; 16 Dome-head screw; 17 Twin-threaded screw

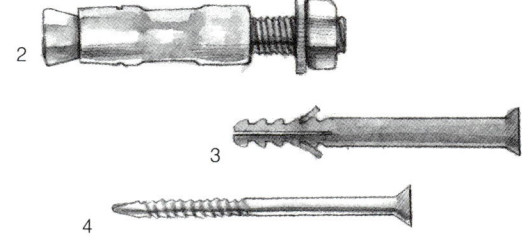

their entire length, giving an excellent grip in wood, and also in fiberboard, particleboard, lumber core, and plywood. The best types are zinc-plated (rust-resistant) and hardened (stronger and less prone to head damage by an ill-fitting screwdriver).

WALL FIXTURES AND BOLTS

The choice of wall fixture depends on the type of wall and the size and weight of the object being attached to it.

Anchors Use a masonry drill bit to drill a hole which matches the size of screw being used (a No 10 bit with a No 10 screw, for example). Insert the anchor in the hole, then insert the screw through the object being fitted and into the anchor. Tighten the screw for a secure attachment.

Solid wall fixtures The method of attaching to a solid brick or block wall is to use an anchor. Traditional fiber anchors have been superseded by plastic versions which will accept a range of screw sizes, typically from No 8 to No 12.

Stud wall fixtures To guarantee a secure fixture, you should locate the lumber uprights (studs) which form the framework of the wall and drive screws into them. If you want to attach something heavy and the lumber uprights are not in the required position, then you must attach horizontal battens to the lumber uprights, since otherwise the fitting will be unsafe.

Cavity-wall fixtures Used on hollow walls, which are constructed from wallboard partition or lath and plaster, which are found in modern and old houses respectively. There are many types of these fixtures including spring toggle, gravity toggle, and nylon toggle, and nearly all of them work on the same principle: expanding wings open up to grip the back of the wallboard or lath and plaster, securing the attachment.

Wall anchor bolt For heavier objects, such as a kitchen unit which will be heavily loaded, a more robust attachment using a wall anchor bolt is advisable. It is similar to an anchor in principle, but has its own heavy-duty machine screw. You need to make a much larger hole in the wall, typically $\frac{3}{8}$in (10mm) in diameter. The sleeve of the anchor expands in the hole as the bolt is tightened and grips the wall firmly.

LATCHES

Magnetic catches Most useful on smaller doors which are unlikely to distort. There must be perfect contact between the magnet fitted to the cabinet frame and the strike plate which is fitted to the door. The other important factor is the pulling power of the magnet – on small cabinet doors a "pull" of $4\frac{1}{2}$–$6\frac{1}{2}$lb (2–3kg) is sufficient. On wardrobe doors an 11–13lb (5–6kg) "pull" is needed.

Magnetic push latches are also useful, especially for small, lightweight doors. Push on the door inwards and it springs open just enough to be grasped and fully opened by the fingers.

Mechanical latches Common types are the spring-loaded ball catch and the roller catch. Again, alignment is vital to success, which is why adjustable types are favored. A mechanical push latch is activated by pressure on the door itself, so a door handle is not necessary.

Peglock catches Particularly suitable for kitchen and bathroom cabinets, where atmospheric conditions can cause doors to warp.

HINGES

The easiest types of hinge to fit are those which do not have to be recessed into the door or door frame – flush, decorative flush (for lightweight doors), or cranked (for cupboard doors). For fitting flaps, piano hinges are used. They are sold in 6ft (1.8m) lengths, and are cut to the required size with a hacksaw. For fitting heavy doors or for

a very neat finish, butt hinges, which are recessed, are a good alternative.

Concealed (or European) hinges are used for particleboard and MDF doors. A special drill bit is required to cut cylindrical holes in the door, but the hinges are adjustable once fitted.

SLIDING DOOR TRACKS

Doors can either be suspended from above or supported from below. The track for glass or panel doors is made from PVC and comes in a variety of colors. The door simply slides along the channel in the track.

Top-hung track Small tongued sliders or adjustable wheel hangers attached to the top edge of the door sit in the track. Small guides keep the bottom edges of the door aligned.

Bottom-roller track The door slides on small rollers located in the track. Guides attached at the top of the door keep it aligned in the track.

TILES

Ceramic tiles Especially popular for kitchens and bathrooms, where durable and waterproof surfaces are essential. There is an enormous range available, and prices vary according to size, shape, and the purpose for which they are required: floor tiles need to be much stronger than wall tiles. Common sizes are $4\frac{1}{4} \times 4\frac{1}{4}$in (108 × 108mm) and 6 × 6in (150 × 150mm), but rectangular shapes are also widely available.

"Universal" tiles have angled edges which ensure that uniform joint spacing is left when the tiles are butted up against each other.

Tiles are sold by the square foot or in boxes of 25 or 50, which will cover one half or one square yard (meter). After calculating the number of tiles required, allow a few extra to cover breakages. Unless you are using only one box, do not use the tiles straight from the box – mix them up with other boxes to disguise any slight color variations.

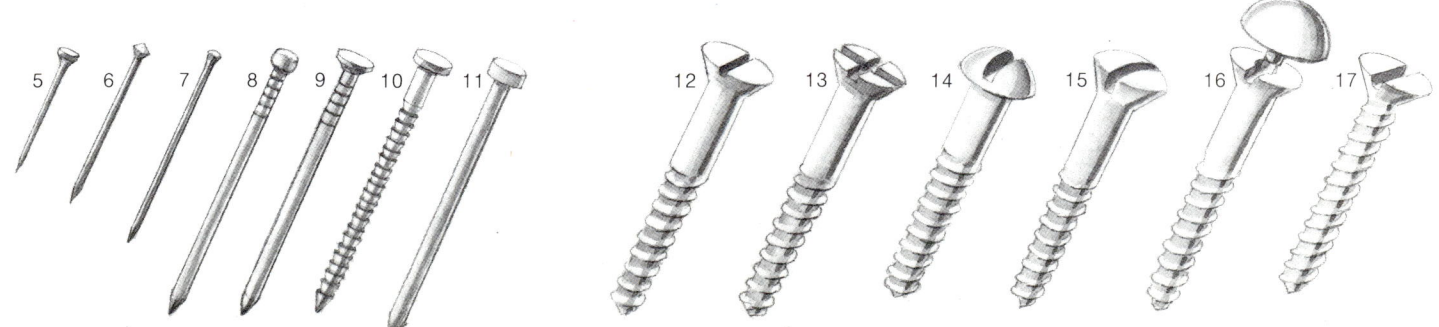

5 6 7 8 9 10 11 12 13 14 15 16 17

TECHNIQUES: SAWING AND CUTTING

WOOD

Wood is available either sawn or planed. Sawn wood is rough in appearance, but is close in width and thickness to the dimensions you specify when ordering. Planed wood is smoothed on all sides, but planing removes $\frac{1}{4}$–$\frac{3}{4}$in (6–19mm) from both the nominal width and the thickness. Sawn wood is ideal for building frameworks, but choose planed wood where a smooth finish is important. Wood should be straight and relatively knot-free. The surface should also be undamaged.

When building a framework of critical thickness you may find it difficult to obtain wood of exactly the required thickness. If so, buy wood that is slightly oversized and ask the lumberyard to plane it down to the size you require.

After building, a fine surface can be obtained by sanding, either by hand with sanding paper wrapped around a sanding block, or by using an electric orbital sander. In both cases, start with medium-grade sanding paper and finish with fine, and only sand in line with the grain, rather than across it, as this can scratch the wood.

Wood finishes If a varnish, wax polish, or paint finish is required, it can be applied easily with a brush (or rag). An alternative, often used by professional furniture makers, is to finish woodwork with a quick-drying cellulose lacquer (see **Materials, page 77**), which can be applied with a paint sprayer. Before spraying, make sure that any holes are filled with stainable wood filler, and stain the surface, if required, before sanding it smooth. The first coat of lacquer is applied as a sealer. Leave it to dry for 30–60 minutes, then rub down the surface with fine sanding paper. Next, apply a second, finishing, coat of lacquer.

MEASURING AND MARKING SQUARE

Mark cutting lines lightly with a hard pencil, then use a utility knife to score against a straight-edge or try square along the rule to create a sharp, splinter-free line.

To mark lumber square, use a try square with the stock (handle) pressed against a flat side of the lumber, called the face side or face edge. Mark a line along the square, using a knife in preference to a pencil, then use the square to mark lines down the edges from the face mark. Finally square the other face side, checking that the lines join up right around the lumber.

Check a try square for accuracy by pressing it against a straight-edge. Mark along the blade, then turn the handle over to see if it aligns with the line from the other side.

If you are measuring and marking a number of pieces of the same length, then clamp them together and mark across several of them at the same time.

SPACING BATTEN

This is simply an offcut of wood, about $\frac{3}{4}$in or 1in square (19mm or 25mm square), which is used to ensure that any slats to be fixed across a frame are spaced an equal distance apart. To ascertain the length to cut the spacing batten, simply bunch all the slats at one end of the frame. Measure to the other end of the frame and divide by the number of spaces (which you can count while you have the slats laid side by side). The resulting measure is the length to cut the spacing batten, which is used to set each slat into its exact position.

BRACING

When making a door or any similar frame, it is vital that it should be square, with corners at perfect right angles. You can ensure this by using one of two bracing methods.

3-4-5 method Measure three units along one rail, four units down the adjacent rail, then nail a bracing batten accurately to one of the unit marks. Pull into square so that the bracing batten measures five units at the other unit mark, forming the long side of a triangle. Saw off the batten ends flush with the frame but do not remove the batten until frame is fitted in place. For large doors such as those on wardrobes, fix two battens on opposing corners.

1 Marking Lumber to Length and Square All Around
Mark across the face of the lumber with a utility knife held against a try square blade. Move knife around corners and mark sides, and finally mark other side to join up the lines.

2 Using Spacing Battens to Space Out Slats Evenly
Bunch the slats together evenly at one end of the frame, then measure to the other end of the frame. Divide this number by the number of spaces required; cut spacing batten(s) to this length.

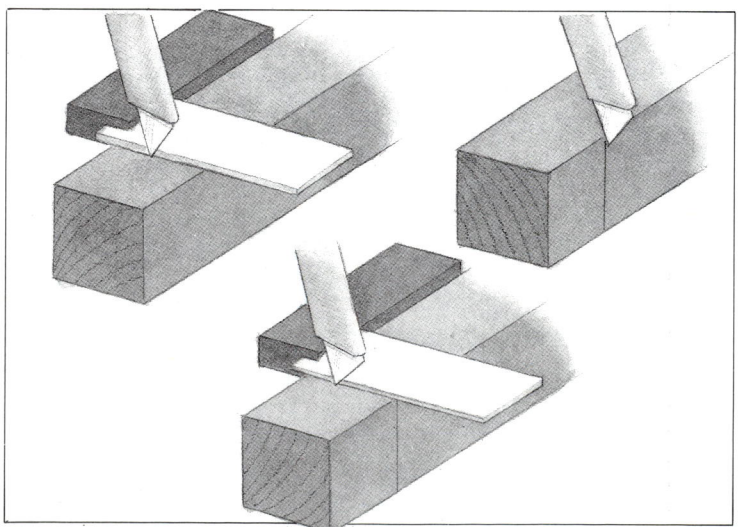

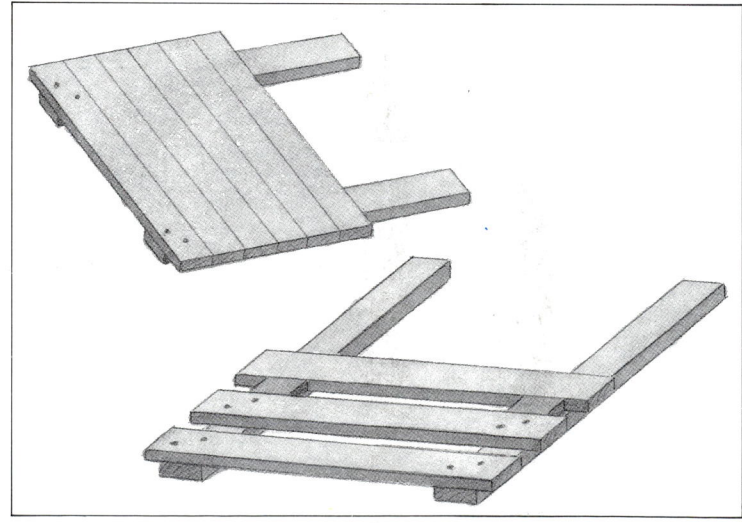

Try square method Nail a batten into one rail, pull into square by using a try square, and then nail the batten into the adjacent rail.

MAKING FOLDING WEDGES

Folding wedges are very useful for clamping large frames on a bench top during assembly. Folding wedges are always used in pairs, but more than one pair may be used to hold a large framework.

Make each pair of wedges from a piece of lumber (hardwood is ideal for this) measuring $1\frac{1}{2}$in × $1\frac{1}{2}$in × 13in (38mm × 38mm × 330mm). Make the wedges by sawing the lumber diagonally into two pieces.

To use the wedges, a wooden batten is first nailed to the bench and the item to be clamped is placed against the batten. Another batten is nailed to the bench, parallel with the first, and about $1\frac{3}{4}$in (45mm) away from the item. The wedges are now placed between the item and the second batten. The ends of the wedges are then knocked inwards with two hammers, thereby clamping the frame.

SAWING AND CUTTING

Cross-cutting to length by hand Hold the lumber firmly with the cutting line (see **Measuring and Marking Square, page 80**) overhanging the right-hand side of the workbench (if you are right-handed). With the saw blade vertical and the teeth on the waste side of the line, draw the handle back to start the cut. To prevent the saw from jumping out of place, hold the thumb joint of your other hand against the side of the saw blade.

Rip-cutting by hand With the lumber or board supported at about knee height, start the cut as described above, then saw down the waste side of the line, exerting pressure on the down cut only. If the saw blade wanders from the line, clamp the edge of a lumber batten exactly above the cutting line on the side to be retained, and saw along it.

Using a portable power saw If the cutting line is only a short distance from a straight edge, adjust the saw's fence so that when it is run along the edge of the lumber, the blade will cut on the waste side of the cutting line. If the lumber is wide, or the edge is not straight, clamp a batten to the surface so that the saw blade will cut on the waste side of the line when it is run along the batten.

Ensuring a straight cut When cutting panels or boards using a power circular saw or a Saber saw, the best way to ensure a straight cut is to clamp a guide batten to the surface of the work, parallel with the cutting line, so that the edge of the base plate can be run along the batten. Obviously, the batten position is carefully adjusted so that the blade cuts on the waste side of the cutting line. Depending on which side of the cutting line the batten is clamped, when using a circular saw, it is possible the motor housing will damage the batten or the C-clamps holding it in place. In this case, replace the batten with a wide strip of straight-edged plywood clamped to the work far enough back for the motor to clear the clamps.

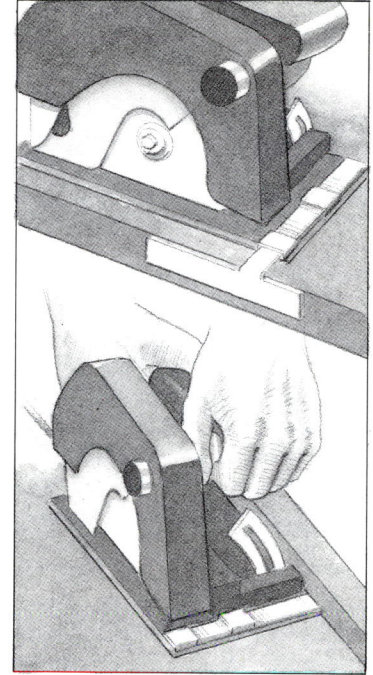

● **Straight Power-saw Cutting**
Top Use the rip fence of the saw if cutting near the edge. *Above* Cutting alongside the batten.

---

❸ **Bracing a Frame Square**
Nail a batten across a corner of the frame so that the 3-4-5 shape triangle is formed.

❹ **Making Folding Wedges**
Saw wood diagonally. Nail batten to bench; wedges fit between batten and item being clamped.

❺ **Cross-cutting to Length**
Hold the lumber firmly. Steady the saw blade with your thumb joint as you start to cut.

❼ **Cutting with a Back Saw**
Start the cut as for a hand saw. As the cut progresses keep the blade horizontal.

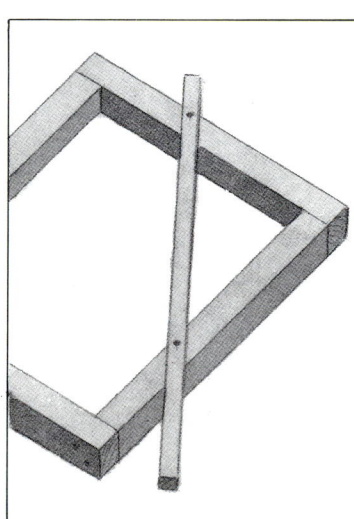

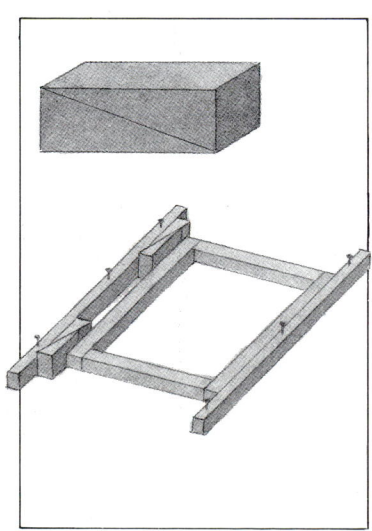

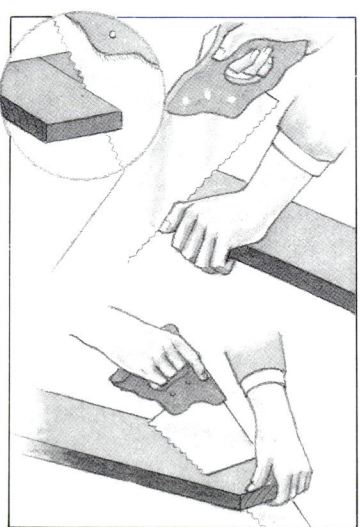

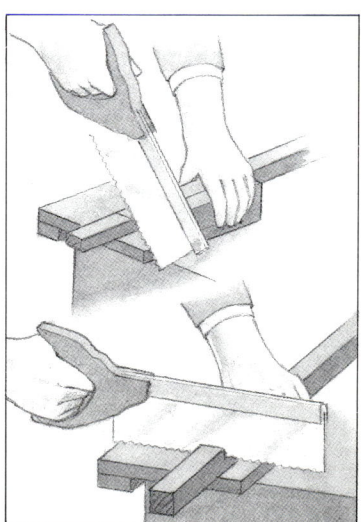

Cutting a Circle

With a Saber saw Mark the circle on the face of the panel. If you do not have a compass, a good makeshift alternative can be made with a loop of string pivoting on a thumb tack at the circle's center. Hold a pencil vertically in the loop at the perimeter to draw the circle.

For a neat, splinter-free edge, carefully score around the cutting line with a sharp utility knife.

To start the cut, drill a hole about $\frac{3}{8}$in (10mm) in diameter just on the waste side of the line. Insert the Saber saw blade through this hole and start the cut from this point, sawing carefully just on the waste side of the cutting line. By scoring the cutting line it will be easier to follow the line and get a smooth edge.

With a coping saw Mark out the circle, score the cutting line, and drill a hole just on the waste side as above. Disconnect the blade from one end of the frame, pass the blade through the hole, and re-connect it to the frame. It will be best to clamp the piece of work vertically when cutting the circle. The blade can be turned in the frame as necessary to help the frame clear the piece of work, but even so, with a coping saw you will be restricted in exactly how far you are able to reach away from the piece of work. If the circle is some way from the edge, use either a power Saber saw or a hand compass saw to cut it.

With a compass saw A compass saw, similar to a keyhole saw, has a stiff, triangular pointed saw blade attached to a simple handle. A very useful compass saw blade is available for fitting in a knife handle.

Because this saw has no frame, it is very useful for cutting circles and other apertures, like keyholes, anywhere in a panel.

Preparation of the circle for cutting, such as marking out, scoring, and drilling for the blade, is the same as for the other methods. When cutting with a compass saw, keep the blade vertical and make a series of rapid, short strokes without exerting too much pressure.

Cutting Curves

The technique is basically the same as for cutting a circle, except that there will be no need to drill a hole in order to start the cut. You can use a Saber saw, coping saw, or compass saw to make the cut. A coping saw is ideal for making this cut because most of the waste can be removed with an ordinary hand saw, since you will be cutting close to the edge of the wood, and the saw frame, therefore, will not get in the way.

Cutting Grooves and Slots

The easiest way to cut grooves (or dados) is to use a router with a bit set to the depth required for the groove. Use a straight-sided router bit. Ideally, the router bit should be the exact width of the groove or slot, so that it can be cut from one setting. If this is not possible, then use a smaller router bit and cut the groove or slot in two or more goes. Make the first cut along the waste side of the line with a batten clamped in line with the groove to guide the base of the router. If a deep groove is required, it may be necessary to make a shallow cut first, then a deeper one.

To cut dados by hand, start by marking out the groove with a utility knife which will ensure a neat finish. Hold the piece of work on a bench, and with a back saw, make vertical cuts just inside the marked lines to the depth of the dado. If the dado is wide, make a series of other vertical cuts in the waste wood. Now chisel out the waste, working from each side to the middle. Finally, with the flat side of the chisel downwards, pare the bottom of the dado so that it is perfectly flat.

Cutting Rabbets

A rabbet is an L-shaped step in the edge of a piece of lumber.

To cut a rabbet by hand, use a marking gauge to mark the rabbet width across the top face of the piece of work and down both sides. Mark the depth of the rabbet across the end and sides.

Hold the lumber flat and saw down on the waste side of the marked line

① Straight Rip-cutting
Clamp a straight batten alongside the cutting line and saw beside the batten. A wedge holds the cut open.

② Using a Power Saber Saw
For a straight cut, clamp a batten alongside line. Cut a circle by following line.

③ Cutting Circles by Hand
1 Drill a small hole and cut circle using a compass saw. *2* Making the cut with a coping saw.

④ Chiseling a Groove
After making saw cuts at side, chisel out waste from each side. Finally pare base flat.

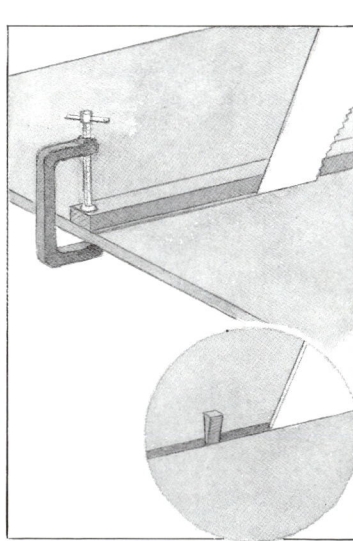
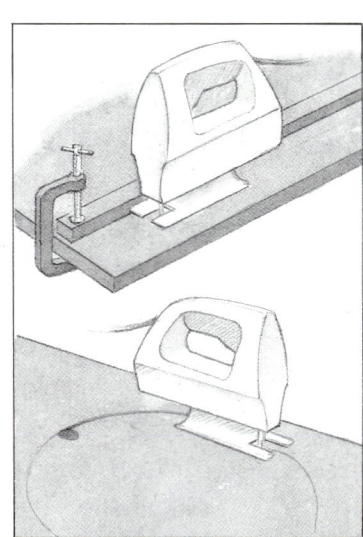
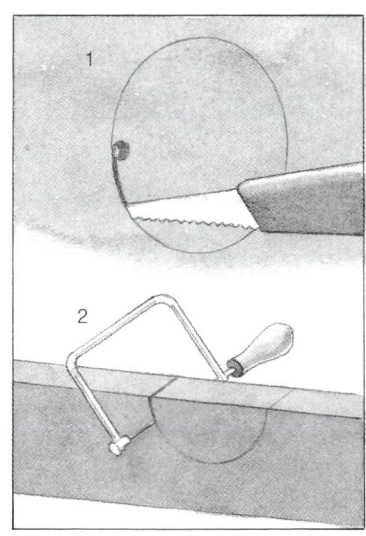

to the depth of the rabbet. Then use a chisel to cut out the waste one bit at a time along the end grain.

It is very easy to cut a rabbet using a router, and in this case it is not necessary to mark out the rabbet unless you want a guide to work to. However, do practice on scrap wood to be sure of setting the router to cut to the correct depth and width.

If using a straight cutter, adjust the guide fence on the router so that the cutter cuts to the correct width, then adjust the cutting depth so that the router will cut to the correct depth. When the router is correctly set up, simply hold it flat on the piece of work and move it against the direction of the cutter's rotation.

If you are using a cutter with a guide pin, simply adjust the depth of cut and then run the cutter along the edge of the wood to form the rabbet. The cutter will follow irregularities in the wood, so make sure the wood is perfectly straight.

MAKING A V-BLOCK

A V-block is useful for holding circular items steady while they are being worked on. Make the block from a length of 2 × 3in (50 × 75mm) S4S lumber – the actual length should be a little longer than the item to be held. The V is made to a depth of about 1in (25mm) in the 3in (75mm) side of the lumber. Cut the V using a circular saw with the blade tilted to 45°. Clamp the block firmly and fit the saw with a guide fence to keep the cut straight. Cut up one side and down the other. Practice on scrap wood while adjusting the depth and width of cut to give the correct size V-shape. Alternatively, you can use a V-cutter bit in a router. It may take two or three passes with the router to make the V to the full depth and width of the cutter.

PLANING

By hand Make sure that the plane blade is sharp and properly adjusted. Stand to one side of the work with your feet slightly apart so you are facing the work and feeling comfortable. Plane from one end of the piece of work to the other, starting the cut with firm pressure on the leading hand, transferring it to both hands, and finally to the rear hand as the cut is almost complete. Holding the plane at a slight angle to the direction of the grain can sometimes improve the cutting action.

With a power plane Remove ties and loose clothing; overalls are ideal. Wear goggles and a painter's mask. Turn the adjuster knob to set the depth to cut and start the plane. Begin with a shallow cut and increase the cutting depth if necessary. Make sure the work is clamped in place.

Stand comfortably to one side of the work and, holding the plane with two hands, set it into the work at one end and pass it over the surface to the other end. Push the plane forwards steadily; not too fast or you will get a wavy surface finish. When you have completed the work, switch off and make sure that the blades stop spinning before resting the plane down with the cutting depth set at zero.

DRILLING

To ensure that screwheads lie flush with the surface of plywood, particleboard or other material use a countersink drill bit.

To minimize the risk of splitting lumber, drill pilot and clearance holes for screws. For small screws, pilot holes can be made with an awl.

The **clearance hole** in the lumber should be fractionally smaller in diameter than the screw shank.

The **pilot hole** in the lumber to receive the screw should be about half the diameter of the clearance hole. The depth of the pilot hole should be slightly less than the length of the screw.

Drilling vertical holes To ensure vertical holes, mount the drill in a drill stand. If this is not possible, stand a try square on edge so that its stock (handle) is resting on the work alongside the drilling position, and the blade is pointing up in the air. Use this as a sighting guide and line up the drill as close as possible with the square to ensure the drill is vertical. It is also helpful if an assistant can stand back and sight along the drill and square from two sides to ensure the drill is held straight.

5 **Making a V-block**
Cut out a V in a block of 2 × 3in (50 × 75mm) lumber using a circular power saw tilted to cut at 45°.

6 **Drilling Vertical Holes**
With a drill stand, not only will the drill bit be held vertical, but depth is also controlled.

7 **Freehand Drilling Guide**
When drilling it can be helpful to stand a try square alongside the drill to ensure accuracy.

8 **Drilling Depth Guide**
There are various guides to control drilling depths, such as rings for drills, and masking tape.

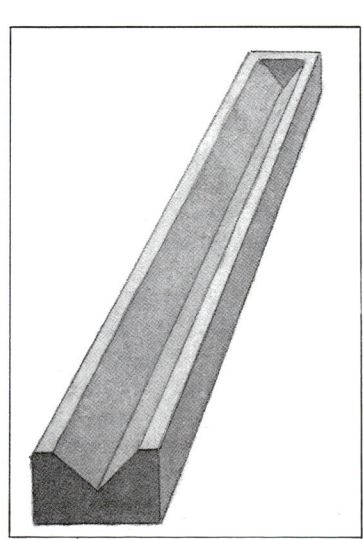

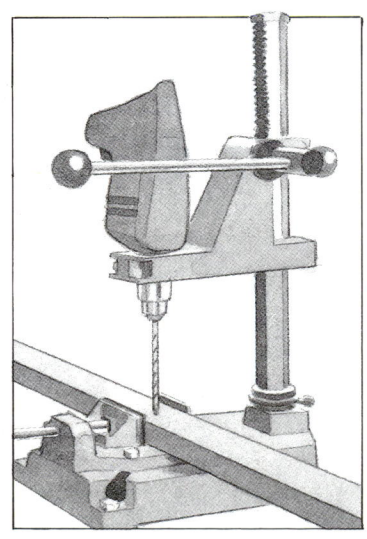

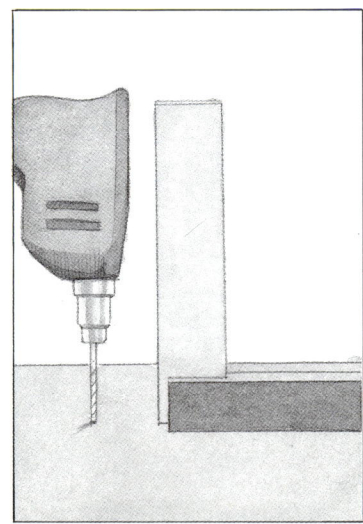

TECHNIQUES: WALL FIXTURES

SCREWING

When screwing one piece of wood to another, make sure that half of the screw penetrates into the bottom piece of wood. The screw's thickness should not exceed one-tenth of the width of the wood into which it has to be inserted. Keep screws at a distance of five times their shank diameter from the side edge of the wood, and ten times the shank diameter from its end.

NAILING

The correct length of nail to use is two-and-a-half to three times the thickness of the lumber being nailed. However, check that the nail will not pierce right through the two pieces being nailed. Wherever possible nail through the thinner piece of wood into the thicker piece.

Nails grip best if driven in at an angle ("**skew nailing**"). A row of nails should be driven in at opposing angles to each other. Framework joints are usually held by skew nailing. Clamp or nail a block of wood temporarily against one side of the vertical piece to stop it sliding as the first nail is started.

To prevent wood from splitting, particularly if nailing near an edge, blunt the points of the nails by hitting them with a hammer before driving them home. Blunt nails will cut through lumber fibers neatly, while pointed nails are more likely to push the fibers apart like a wedge, leading to splitting.

WALL FIXTURES

Solid wall The normal attachment for a solid wall is a wood screw and plastic anchor. Before drilling the fixing hole, check with a metal detector that there are no pipes or cables hidden below the surface. Drill the holes for the anchor with a masonry drill bit in an electric drill. The anchor packing will indicate the drill size to use. Switch to hammer action if the wall is hard. The screw should be long enough to go through the fixture and into the wall by about 1in (25mm) if the masonry is exposed, and by about $1\frac{3}{8}$in (35mm) into a plastered wall.

If the wall crumbles when you drill into it, mix up a cement-based plugging compound (available from home improvement stores). Turn back the screw half a turn before the compound sets (in about five minutes). When it is hard (in about one hour) the screw can be removed and a heavy attachment made.

If your drill sinks easily into the wall once it has penetrated the plaster layer, and a light gray dust is produced from the hole, you are fixing into lightweight concrete blocks. In this case, special winged anchors for soft blocks should be used.

To make a quick, light-to-medium weight attachment in a solid wall, a masonry nail can be used. Choose a length that will penetrate the material to be attached, and pierce an exposed masonry wall by $\frac{5}{8}$in (16mm) and a plastered wall by about 1in (25mm). Wear goggles in case the hardened nail snaps when you strike it, and hammer it gently through the material to be attached and into the wall.

Lath and plaster For a strong attachment, screw directly into the main vertical studs to which the laths are nailed. You can find these studs with a metal detector (see **Stud wall**, below).

For a lightweight attachment you can screw into the wood laths. These can be located by probing with a pointed implement such as an awl. Then insert a twin-thread wood screw. For medium-to-heavyweight attachments into lath and plaster, drill between the laths and use a cavity-wall fitting suitable for lath and plaster, such as a spring toggle, gravity toggle, or nylon toggle.

Stud wall For a strong attachment into a gypsum wallboard-covered stud wall, make a screw fixing directly into the vertical studs. You can find these by tapping the wall to check where it sounds most dense, and then probing these areas with a pointed implement until a firm background is found. Alternatively, you can make a small hole in the wall, and push a stiff wire into it horizontally until an obstruction is felt, which will be the stud. Withdraw the wire and hold it on the surface of

---

① Drilling Holes for Screws in Lumber
Drill a clearance hole in the thinner piece. Countersink this hole, then drill a hole to slightly less than screw length. _Inset_ To counterbore, drill to the diameter of the screwhead to required depth, then as above.

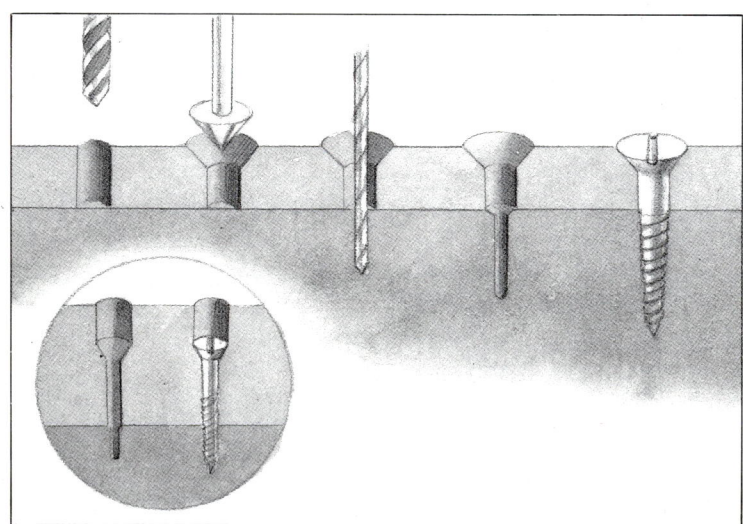

② Techniques for Joining Wood by Nailing
Nail should be two-and-a-half to three times the thickness of the lumber being joined. Assemble frames on bench by nailing against batten. _Inset_ Blunt nail points to avoid splitting lumber.

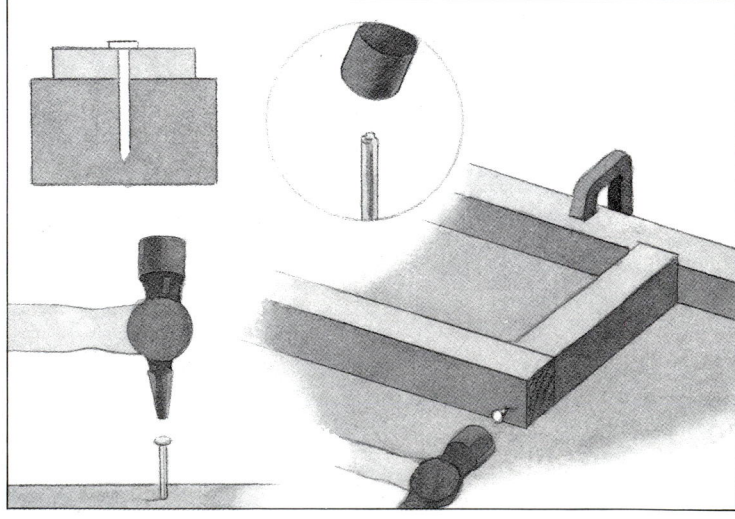

the wall so that the edge of the stud can be marked. By drilling about 1in (25mm) to the farther side of this mark, the center of the stud will be found and a screw can be inserted.

To avoid making holes in the surface of a wall, a metal detector can be used. Move it over the wall to locate a pattern of nails and mark this on the surface. Vertical rows of nails indicate a stud. Alternatively, use one of the newer electronic stud and joist detectors. This is moved over the surface to detect a change in density between the different construction materials. A change indicates the position of a stud.

If a fixture cannot be made into a stud, a lighter fixture can be made into gypsum wallboard by using a fixture designed for that material. Follow the manufacturer's instructions for the size of hole required, which can be made in gypboard with an ordinary twist drill bit.

Cavity wall Cavity walls comprise a solid inner leaf of bricks or concrete blocks surfaced with plaster and separated from the outer leaf of bricks or stone blocks by a cavity about 2in (50mm) wide.

When tapped, a cavity wall sounds solid. For fixtures, treat it is a solid wall (see page 84).

BEVELED BATTENS

These provide a very secure method of holding heavy objects on to a wall. The battens are formed by sawing a strip of wood lengthways with the saw blade set at 45°. This results in two interlocking pieces of wood. One piece, with the sloping face pointing upwards and the narrower face facing the wall, is screwed to the wall. The other piece, with the sloping face pointing downwards and the narrower side facing the item to be hung, is screwed to the item to be attached. When the item is lifted into place, the battens interlock and produce a very secure attachment.

For security, the battens should be formed by sawing a 1 × 4in (25 × 100mm) strip of lumber lengthways. Screws should be applied to the wall and into the item to be hung at about 8in (200mm) intervals. Use No 10 wood screws – 1½in (38mm) long into the item to be hung, and 2½in (65mm) long into the wall. Anchors will also be required.

ATTACHING RIGHT-ANGLED BRACKETS

These are right-angled steel strips pre-drilled for screw fixing and are useful for attaching lumber frames to walls and ceilings, as long as the brackets are positioned out of sight.

Decide where you want the bracket, hold it in place on the frame and use a pencil to mark the center of one screw fixing position. Drill a pilot hole and attach the bracket with one screw. Repeat for the other brackets. Position the frame and check that it is vertical. Mark center points of the bracket fixing holes on the wall or ceiling. Remove the frame and use a masonry drill to make anchor holes at the required positions. Press anchors into holes. Before replacing the frame and screwing brackets in place, check that brackets are still accurately positioned on the frame. Drill pilot holes for the remaining screw fixings, and insert the screws.

③ **Skew Nailing for Strength**
Assemble frames by skew nailing (driving nails at an angle). The joint will not then pull apart.

④ **Using a Nailset**
For a neat finish, use a nailset to drive nail heads below the surface, then fill indentation.

⑤ **Using Beveled Battens**
For a secure fixing on a wall use beveled battens made by sawing a batten lengthwise at 45°.

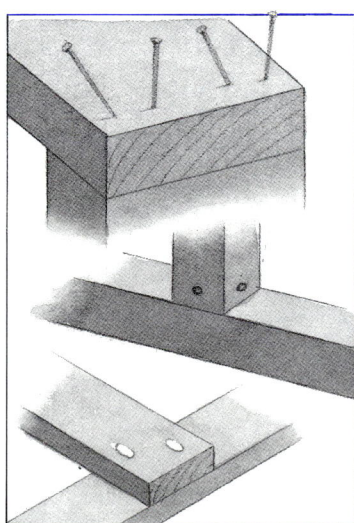

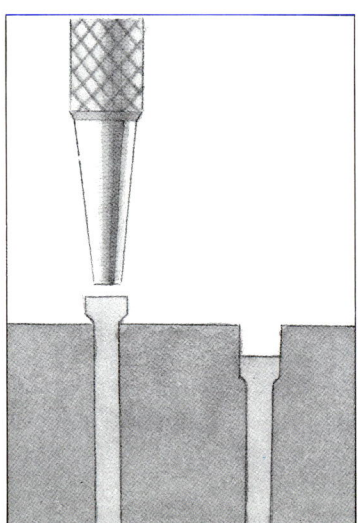

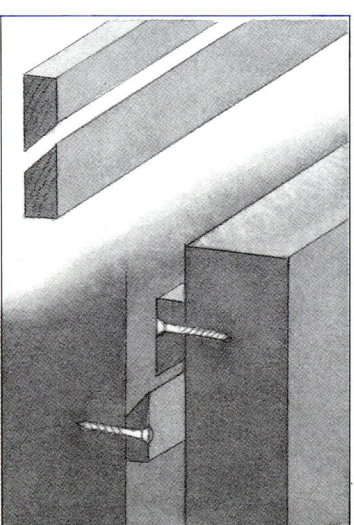

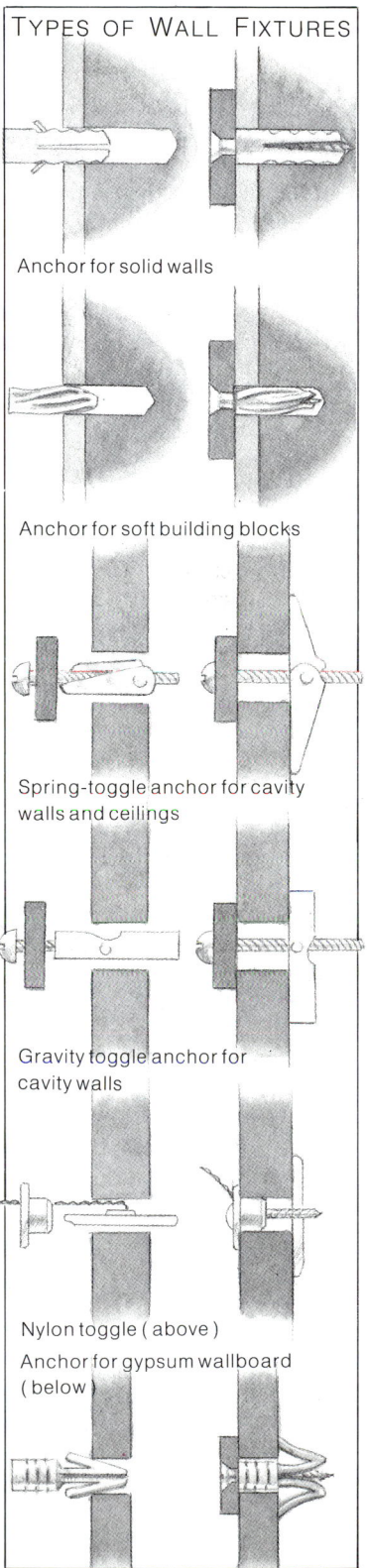

TYPES OF WALL FIXTURES

Anchor for solid walls

Anchor for soft building blocks

Spring-toggle anchor for cavity walls and ceilings

Gravity toggle anchor for cavity walls

Nylon toggle (above)
Anchor for gypsum wallboard (below)

WOOD JOINTS

Butt joint This is the simplest frame joint of all. The ends of the lumber to be jointed must be cut square so that they butt together neatly. Corner and "T" joints can be formed, which are glued and nailed for strength. Corrugated fasteners can also be used to hold these joints, especially where the sides of the frames will be covered to hide the fasteners. When "T" joints are being formed from inside a frame, they can be skew nailed (see page 84).

Corner joint This is a simple "knock down" fixture attached with screws; it is used to attach boards at right angles. They are described as "knock down" joints because some are in two parts for easy disassembly, and even the simple attachments can be unscrewed. They do not look very attractive, but are useful where they will be hidden – by a fascia, for example.

Miter joint Popular for making picture frames, but suitable for other right-angled corner joints. Cut the joint at 45° using a miter box as a guide. A simple miter joint is glued and nailed, but a stronger joint can be made using dowels, or by making oblique saw cuts into which wood veneers are glued.

Half-lap joint Also known as halving joints, these join wood of similar thickness at corners or to form "T" or "X" joints (mid-lap and cross-lap joints). Cut each piece to half its thickness. Use a try square to mark the width of the cut-outs and a marking gauge set to half the thickness of the wood to mark their depth. Be sure to cross-hatch the waste wood with a pencil so that the correct side is removed. To form an end-lap joint, saw down as for making a tenon joint (see page 88). To form a mid- or cross-lap, saw down on each side of the "T" cut-out to the depth of the central gauge line, then chisel out the waste.

Dado joint Used mainly for shelving, this is basically a slot into which a shelf fits. The "through" dado joint

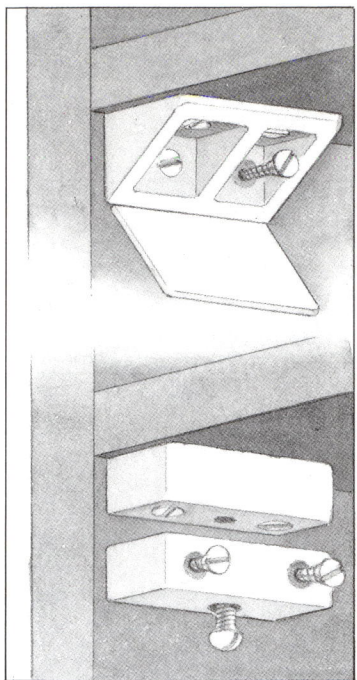

② Corner Fitting Joints
Ideal for joining wood and boards at right angles. *Top* A one-piece fitting. *Bottom* A two-part type. Both are easily fitted using screws.

⑤ Cutting Miter Joints
Miters make right-angled corner joints. Using a miter box as a guide for ensuring a 45° angle, cut out the joint with a back saw.

① Simple Butt Joints
Top Corner and *below* "T" joints can be formed by skew nailing or by using corrugated fasteners.

③ Types of Half-lap Joints
Top A corner-lap joint. *Bottom left* A mid-lap joint. *Bottom right* A cross-lap joint.

④ Forming a Half-lap Joint in Lumber Battens
Mark width of the cut-out. Mark half the thickness of the wood with a marking gauge. Cross hatch area to be removed. Saw down sides with a back saw, then chisel out the waste.

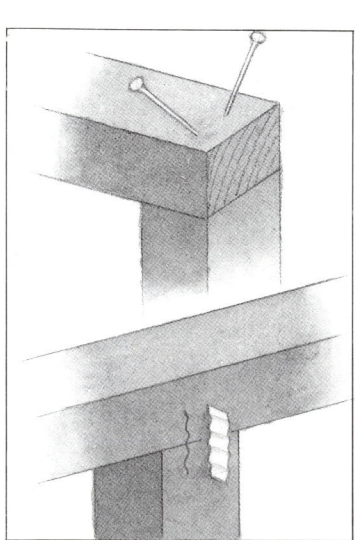

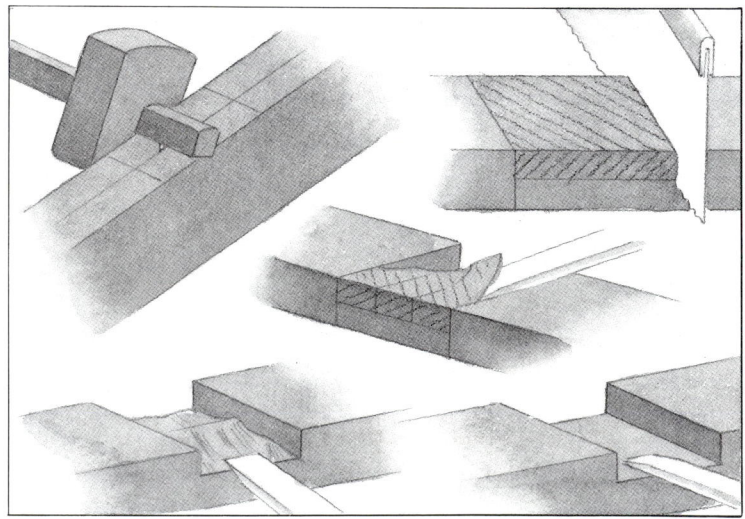

goes to the full width of the shelf, while a "stopped" dado joint is taken only part of the way across the board. Chisel the waste away from each side. In the case of a stopped dado, chisel the waste from the stopped end first. If you have a router, it is easier to cut a dado joint by running the router across the board against a batten clamped at right angles to the board to guide the router accurately.

A rabbet joint is similar to a dado joint at the top of a board, and can be cut in a similar way (see **Cutting rabbets, page 82**).

Bare-faced rabbet-and-dado joint This type of dado joint, used at the corners of a frame, is a much stronger joint than the common butt joint or lap joint because the rabbet of one piece is held in a dado cut in the other piece. The joint will be held just with good aliphatic resin wood-working glue, and by nailing or screwing down through the top into the upright. However, because of the short grain of the outside of the dado, this piece is left overlong while

the joint is made, and then the "horn" (the excess timber) is cut off neatly, flush with the side of the joint. The rabbet should be no thicker than half the width of the lumber being jointed.

Carefully mark out the joint with a utility knife, a try square, and a marking gauge. The depth of the dado (groove) should be about one-third to a half the thickness of the upright. Cut the sides of the dado to the required depth using a back saw held vertical, or a carefully set circular saw. Clamping a batten alongside the dado will help to keep the cut straight. Remove the waste with a chisel, working from both sides to the middle, and holding the chisel with the flat side downwards. Alternatively, cut the dado with a router (see **Cutting grooves and slots, page 82**).

Mark out the vertical piece so that the rabbet will exactly fit in the dado. Use a marking gauge to mark out the rabbet. The rabbet is cut with a router or with a hand saw and chisel to form the tongue (see **Cutting rabbets, page 82**).

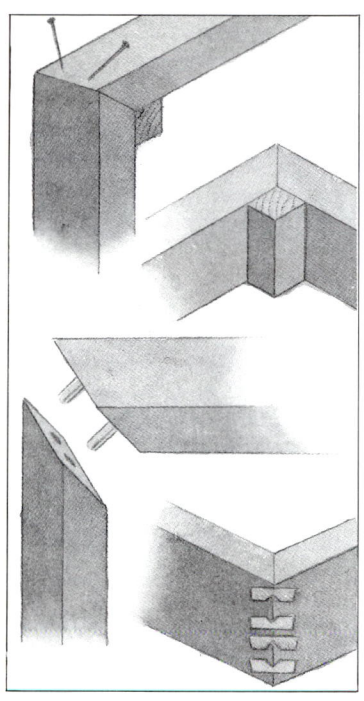

6 Forming Miter Joints
Top Glue and nail together a simple miter joint. *Bottom* Reinforce the joint with a corner block, dowels, or wood veneer.

8 Types of Dado Joint
Top A through dado joint. *Middle* A through dado joint on the side of a central support. *Bottom* A corner dado joint.

7 Stages in Forming a Through Dado Joint
Mark width of the dado according to the thickness of the wood being joined. Use a utility knife. Mark depth with a marking gauge. Cut down the sides with a back saw. Chisel out the waste, working from both sides to the middle.

9 Stages in Making a Bare-faced Rabbet-and-dado Joint
Leave a "horn" of surplus lumber to support the short grain which will be on the outside of the groove. Mark width of piece being joined. Mark and cut dado as before. Saw off horn.

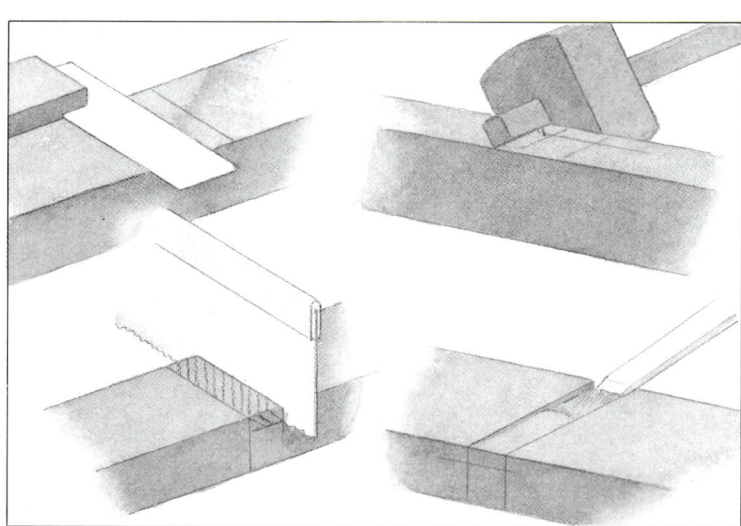

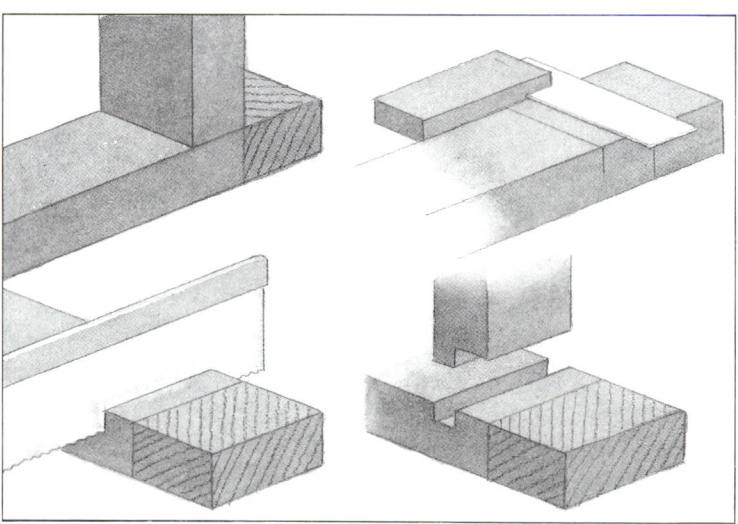

TECHNIQUES: WOOD JOINTS

Mortise and tenon joint A mortise and tenon joint can be marked out with a mortise gauge. Mark out the tenon (the tongue) so that it is one-third of the thickness of the piece of wood. The mortise (the slot) is marked at the same width in the other piece. The length of the mortise should match the width of the tenon being fitted. Drill out most of the waste with a series of holes using a drill bit slightly smaller than the mortise width. Working from the center, chop out the mortise with a chisel to the depth required. If making a through joint (in which the end of the tenon is visible), turn the wood over and complete the mortise from the other side.

Hold the tenon piece upright, but sloping away from yourself, secure in a vise, and use a back saw carefully to cut down to the shoulder. Then swivel the wood around to point the other way, and saw down to the other side of the shoulder. Next, position the wood vertically and cut down to the shoulder. Finally, place the wood flat and saw across the shoulder to remove the

2 Marking and Cutting a Mortise and Tenon Joint
Mark the length of the mortise slot to match the size of the rail being joined. Set the mortise gauge to the width of the chisel being used to cut out the mortise slot. (Chisel should be about one-third the width of wood being joined.) Use the mortise gauge to mark the mortise, and also the tenon, on the rail. Drill out the mortise and complete the cut with a chisel. Use a back saw to cut out the tenon.

1 Mortise and Tenon Joints
Top A common or stopped mortise and tenon joint. *Below* Through mortise and tenon joint.

3 Making a Haunched Mortise and Tenon Joint
Leave rail over-long. Mark out as before but allow for shoulder at top. Cut mortise slot, then saw down sides of a shoulder. Finish mortise using a chisel. Cut tenon as shown.

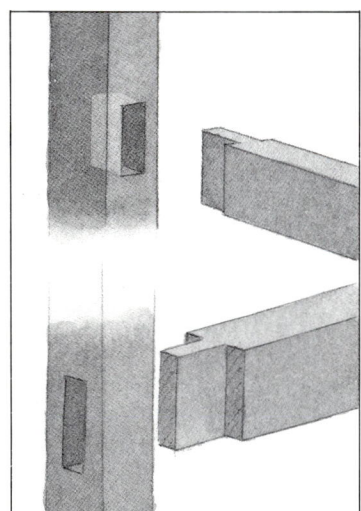

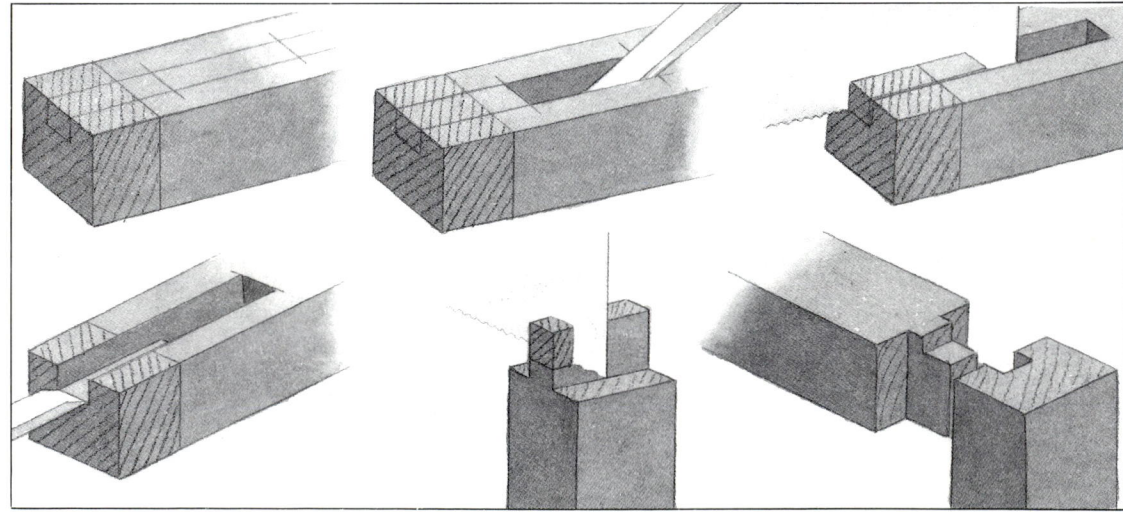

waste. Repeat for the waste on the other side of the tongue. Check that the two pieces fit well before gluing and assembling the joint. For added strength and a better appearance, cut small additional shoulders at each end of the tenon. If made accurately, these joints will withstand a lot of wear, and are capable of supporting a heavy load.

Haunched mortise and tenon joints For joints at the corner of a large frame, or for joints that will have to support heavy weights, a square "haunch" or shoulder can be left in the tenon to increase its effective width and considerably strengthen the joint.

The joint is marked out with a try square, utility knife, and marking gauge as for an ordinary mortise and tenon, but allowance is made for a square shoulder at the top as shown in the diagram.

To prevent the small amount of cross-grain lumber above the mortise from being pushed out when the mortise slot is cut, the rail is left overlong at this stage to create a "horn"

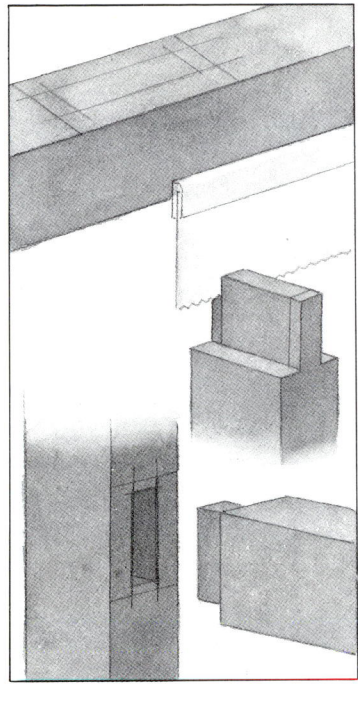

⑤ Shouldered Tenon Joint
For enhanced strength and appearance, cut small additional shoulders at each end tenon. Do this by sawing down.

④ Making a Bare-faced Mortise and Tenon Joint
Tenon is offset to one side. Mark and cut as shown here.

which is cut off after the joint has been made and assembled.

Bare-faced mortise and tenon joint If the tongue of a tenon joint is offset to one side, this produces a bare-faced tenon as shown below (fig 4). This produces a strong joint which is very useful in cases where narrow rails meet the thicker rails of the main frame. The mortise slots in the frame rails can be cut farther back from the front edge for extra strength, and the bare-faced tenons of the narrow rails allow the front faces of these rails to lie flush with the front face of the main frame, giving a neat, secure finish.

A bare-faced tenon is cut in the same way as a half-lap joint (or halving joint).

Dovetail joint A dovetail joint is made so that the "pins," which are the protruding fingers, interlock in both parts of the joint, giving a joint of great pull-out strength. The joint can only come apart in the same way as it was assembled.

A sliding bevel is used to mark out

a central dovetail pin on one rail, and the dovetail shape is cut out using a dovetail saw or fine-toothed back saw to leave a central pin.

The thickness and shape of the pin is marked on the other piece, called the "post," and the marks are extended on to the ends using a try square. The post is held upright and the waste inside the two outer pins is cut out using a dovetail saw, while a coping saw is used to cut across the bottom of the waste. The sides are pared down to size with a chisel.

⑥ Marking Out and Cutting a Dovetail Joint
Mark a line the thickness of the matching piece. Using a mortise gauge, mark top of the pin. Mark sides of pin with sliding bevel set at slope of 1 in 6. Cut pin with back saw. Hold pin on other piece. Mark dovetail and cut out waste with back and coping saws. Pare base accurately with chisel to achieve good fit.

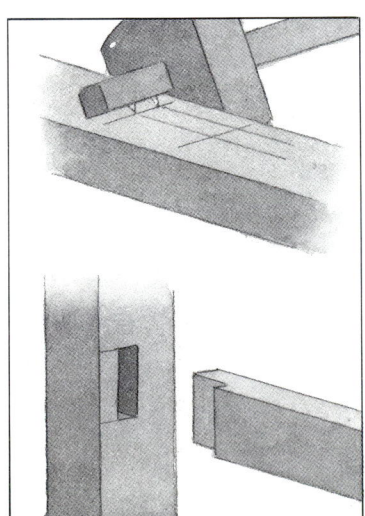

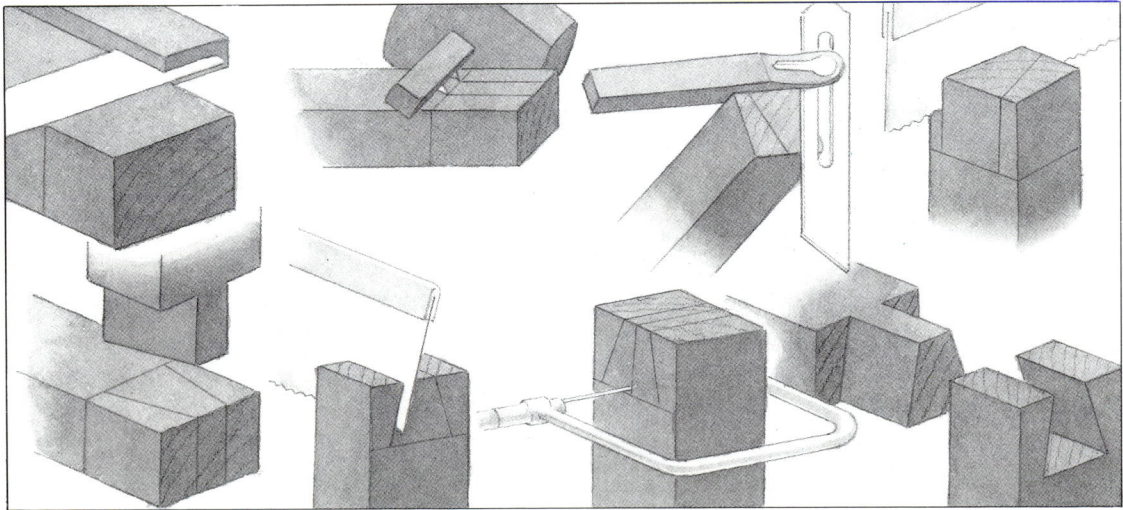

Dowel joint Dowels are a strong, simple, and hidden means of joining wood together.

Use pre-cut grooved dowels with beveled ends (see **Materials, page 78**). These range from $\frac{1}{4}$in (6mm) diameter by 1in (25mm) long to $\frac{3}{8}$in (10mm) by 1$\frac{1}{2}$in (38mm). The dowel length should be about one-and-a-half times the thickness of the wood being jointed. If you need to use doweling of a larger diameter (as used in the cupboard door frames in the Tiled Kitchen or for the Alcove Shelves and Cupboards), cut your own lengths of dowel. Cut grooves down the length of dowel to allow glue and air to escape, and bevel the ends. The dowel lengths should be twice the thickness of the wood being joined.

On both pieces of wood, use a marking gauge to find the center line, and mark with a pencil. Drill the dowel holes to half the dowel length with the drill held in a drill stand, or aligned with a try square stood on end. Drill the dowel holes in one of the pieces to be jointed, insert center points in the holes, then bring the two pieces of the joint together so they are carefully aligned. The center points will make marks in the second piece of wood where the dowel holes should be drilled. Drill the holes to half the length of the dowels, plus a little extra for glue. Where dowels are used for location rather than strength, such as for joining worktops, set the dowels three-quarters into one edge and a quarter into the other.

Put glue in the holes and tap the dowels into the holes in the first piece with a mallet. Apply glue to both parts of the joint; bring them together and clamp them in position until the glue has set.

GLUING

All joints are stronger if glued. Make sure that surfaces to be joined are clean and well-fitting. Clamp surfaces together while the glue is setting, but not so tightly that all the glue is squeezed from the joint. Use waterproof glue for joints that may be subject to dampness. If the parts do not fit tightly, use a two-part resorcinol glue.

1 Types of Dowel Joint
Dowels can join panels edge to edge and join frames at corners. They can be hidden or have ends exposed.

2 Dowels to Join Panels
Right Mark dowel positions. Drill holes, insert center points. Mark second piece.

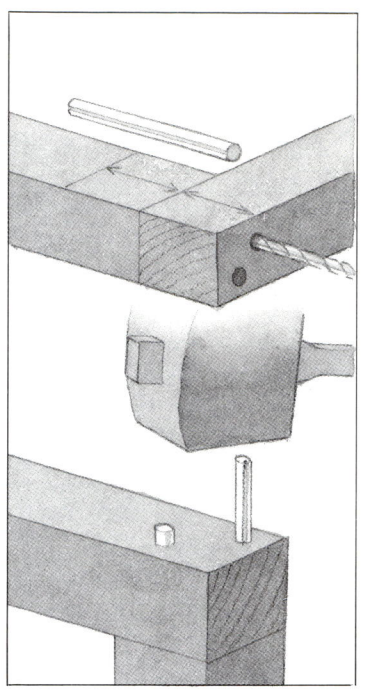

3 Making a Doweled Frame
If edge of frame will not be seen, drill holes for dowels after making frame. Hammer dowels home; cut ends flush after glue dries.

4 Using a Doweling Jig
If dowels are to be hidden, a doweling jig makes it easy to drill holes that align in both pieces.

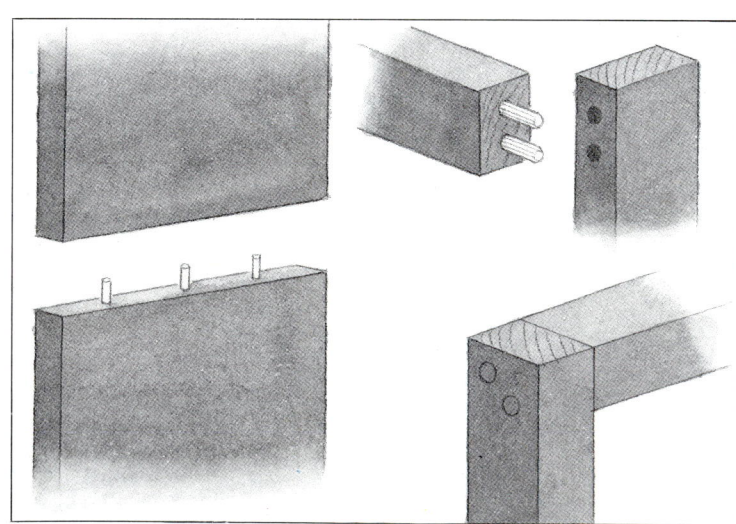

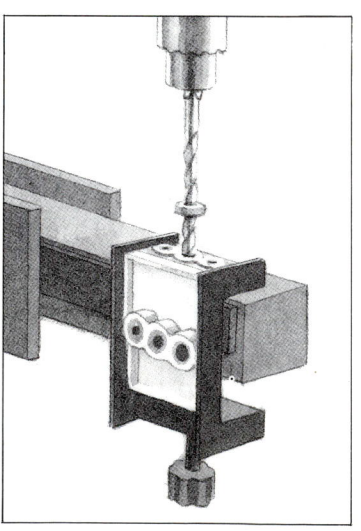

SCRIBING AND LEVELING

Scribing long lengths When you are fitting a worktop, horizontal panel, shelf, or vertical panel to a wall, you are likely to find that it will not touch the wall at every point since it is extremely unlikely that the wall will be flat and square. To avoid such gaps, it is necessary to scribe the item to the wall.

Hold the item in place and as close to its final position as possible. If it is a worktop, make sure that it is level and at right angles to whatever is next to it. If it is an upright, make sure that the front edge is held plumb. Where the gap is at its widest, pull the panel forward so that the gap is 1in (25mm). Take a block of wood 1in (25mm) long and place it on the panel, against the wall, at one end. Hold a pencil against the other end of the block, and draw the pencil and block along the wall so that the pencil makes a line, which reproduces the contours of the wall.

With a Saber saw or a compass saw, cut along the line. Where the line is too close to the edge to saw,

shape the panel to the line using a tool such as a Surform or a wood rasp. Press the panel against the wall and check that it fits neatly all the way along.

Scribing in alcoves It is more difficult to scribe in an alcove because a horizontal panel will usually fit neatly only *after* it has been scribed to the walls.

Using a large wooden square (you can make one from lumber battens following the 3-4-5 principle of producing a right-angled triangle [*see* page 80]), find out if one, or both, of the side walls are square and flat. If they are, you can carefully measure between them at the required height of the worktop. Then saw off the ends of the worktop to this length and position it, before finally scribing it to the rear wall as described above.

If the side walls of the alcove are not square, you can mark out the worktop using a cardboard template (*see* **Using templates**) of each side wall and part of the rear wall which you then scribe to fit.

Using a contour gauge This device (*see* **Tools, page 72**) is used for reproducing a complicated shape and is useful if you have to fit, for example, a worktop around something such as a decorative wood molding. It comprises a row of movable pins or narrow plastic strips held in place by a central bar. When pressed against a shape, the pins follow the outline of the shape. The contour gauge is then held on the item to be fitted and the shape transferred to it by drawing around the contour gauge with a pencil. After use, realign the pins.

Using templates When cutting around an awkward-shaped object, such as a pipe, it is a good idea to make a template of the obstruction. Make the template from cardboard or thick paper. Cut and fold the template to make it as accurate as you can. When you are satisfied that you have a good fit, place the template on the item to be fitted, and mark around it to produce a cutting line. Alternatively, glue the template in position and cut around it.

Leveling battens When attaching battens to a wall with masonry nails, first lay the battens on the floor and drive the nails almost all the way through them. On the wall, use a carpenter's level to position the batten horizontally and draw a pencil line along the top edge of the batten. Hold the batten in position and drive a masonry nail at one of the ends part of the way into the wall. Check that the top of the batten aligns with the guide line, then rest the carpenter's level on the batten and, with the bubble central, drive a nail into the wall at the other end of the batten. Make sure that the batten is level, then drive in all the nails.

If attaching the batten with screws, drill clearance holes in the batten as above and, with a pointed tool, mark the wall through a screw hole at one end of the batten. Drill and anchor the wall at this point (*see* **Wall fixtures, page 84**) then screw the batten to the wall. Level the batten as above, mark the other screw positions, then remove the batten and drill and anchor the wall. Finally, screw the batten in place.

⑤ Scribing Long Lengths to Fit Against a Wall
Where gap is widest pull panel forwards so gap is 1in (25mm). Hold pencil against 1in (25mm) wide block; move block and pencil along wall to draw cutting line. Cut along this line.

⑥ Attaching Leveling Battens to a Wall
If attaching with masonry nails drive these into battens first. Hold batten in place and mark wall. Holding batten on marked line, insert nail at end. Recheck level; drive in other nails.

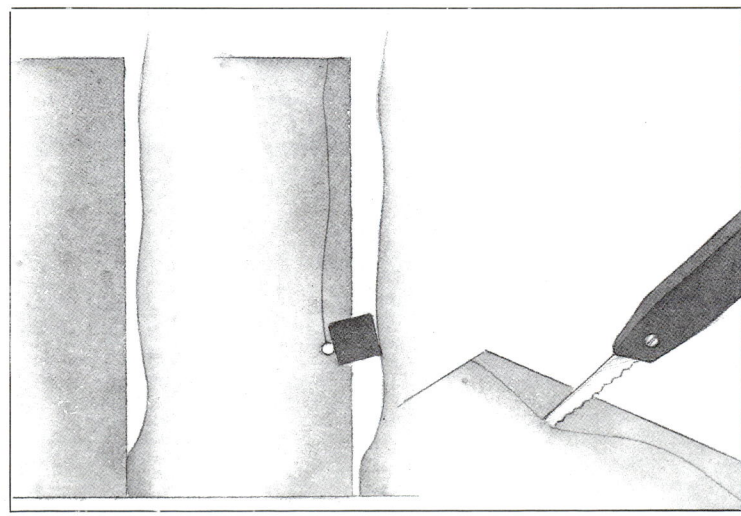

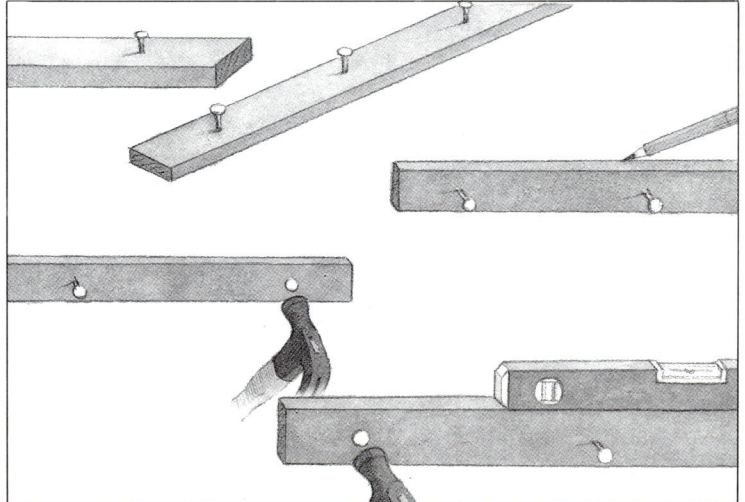

TECHNIQUES: FITTING DOORS AND HINGES

Leveling units Floors are rarely level, so that when installing the alcove cupboard frame you must work from the highest spot in the room. Assemble the units and temporarily place them in position. Take a long, straight wooden batten and place this on the top of the units. Place a carpenter's level on the horizontal batten, to find the highest unit. Work from this unit and bring all the other units up to this level by shimming pieces of plywood or hardboard underneath them. After this is done, the top can be installed, and the doors and shelves fitted.

Alternatively, if you have yet to construct the support units, you can build each one to the exact height required to compensate for differences in floor level. This leveling technique is very useful for old properties where floors are invariably uneven. First, lay straight battens around the floor where the units will be positioned – one batten at the front edge and one at the back. Work from the high point and shim the battens so that they are level. Mark on them the positions of the units and at each point measure the gap to the floor. Increase the height of each unit by this amount.

Finding verticals Use a plumb line to mark a vertical line on a wall. Tap a nail into the wall where you want the vertical to be, and tie the plumb line to it. When the line is steady, hold a scrap of wood on the wall so it just touches the string and mark the wall at this point. Repeat the procedure at a couple of other places. Alternatively, rub the plumb line with chalk. When it stops swinging, press it against the wall, then pluck the string to leave a vertical chalk line on the wall.

HANGING DOORS

Hinged cupboard or wardrobe doors There are two ways to fit hinged doors; they can be **inset** to fit between side frames, or they can be **flush overlay** where the doors cover the side frames.

Inset doors look attractive, but they are harder to fit than flush overlay doors because they must be very accurately made to achieve a uniform gap all round the opening. Flush overlay doors cover the frame and hide any uneven gaps. Also, the concealed hinges that are normally used to hang a flush overlay door are adjustable, making it easy to alter the door so that it opens and closes correctly.

Sliding cupboard and wardrobe doors Small doors slide in double U-channel tracks made from lumber or plastic. Shallow U-channel track is fitted along the bottom front edge of the opening and a deeper track is fitted at the top, to the underside of the front edge. The grooves in the track should match the door thickness and it is important to fit the top track exactly vertically above the bottom track. Make sliding doors so that they overlap each other by about $1\frac{3}{4}$–2in (45–50mm). Their height should be the distance from the bottom to the groove in the top track, plus $\frac{1}{4}$in (6mm). After assembly of the frame unit, the door can be fitted by lifting it up and into the top track, and then slotting it into the bottom track.

Heavier doors must be hung using an overhead- or bottom-track roller system. Fitting is usually straightforward if you follow the manufacturer's instructions. Even if the track has not been fixed exactly horizontal, there is usually a means of adjusting the doors so that they move and close smoothly.

FITTING HINGES

Inset doors **Flush hinges** are the easiest to fit. They are simply screwed to the edge of the door and the frame, and require no recessing. However, they cannot be adjusted after fitting. The inner flap of the hinge is screwed to the edge of the door, while the outer flap is screwed to the inner face of the frame.

Attach the hinges at equal distances from the top and bottom of the door. With a tall or very heavy door, fit a third hinge centrally between the other two. Mark the hinge positions on the edge of the door with the hinge knuckle (joint) in line with the door front. Drill pilot holes and screw on the inner flap. Hold the door in place or rest it on something

① Using a Contour Gauge
To reproduce complicated shapes, press the gauge against objects; use it as a pattern.

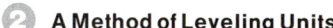

② A Method of Leveling Units
Temporarily position the units or the partition frame. Place carpenter's level on a straight batten to find the highest unit. Pack plywood or hardwood pieces under other units to bring them to this height.

③ Fitting Sliding Door Track
Heavy doors are best hung on bottom track. Track screws to floor and rollers are inset in door bottoms.

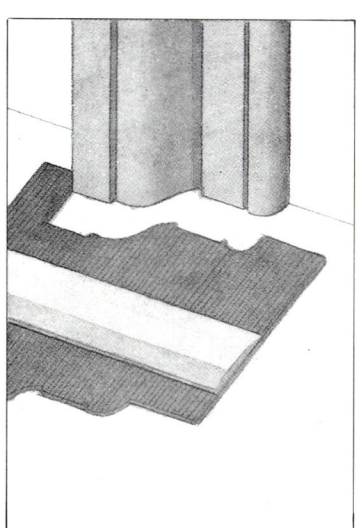

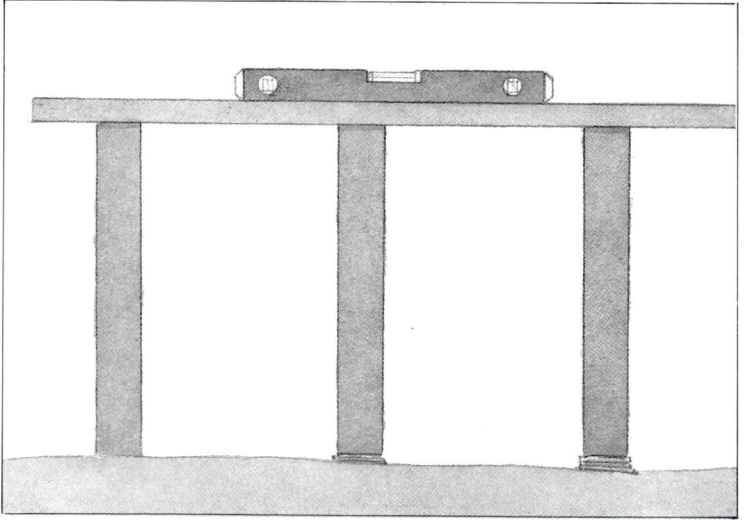

to raise it to the correct height, making sure that it is accurately aligned at the top and bottom, and mark the positions of the hinges on the frame. Remove the door and extend these lines using a try square. Hold the door against the frame so it is in an open position, and screw the outer hinge flaps in place, so that they match up with the guide lines.

Butt hinges are conventional flapped hinges and are available in steel (commonly) or in brass, which is better for high quality work. They are attached in the same way as flush hinges, except that the hinge flaps have to be recessed into the lumber using a chisel or router.

Mark out the hinge positions as for flush hinges, making sure that the hinges are not positioned so that the fixing screws will go into the end grain of cross members and be likely to pull out.

The length of the hinges are marked out first, using a utility knife, then the width of the hinge and the thickness of the flap are marked using a marking gauge. With a chisel held vertical, and a mallet, cut

down around the waste side of the recess, then make a series of vertical cuts across the full width of the recess. Remove the waste by careful chiseling, then finally pare the bottom of the recess flat using the chisel held flat-side downwards.

If you are careful, you can remove the bulk of the waste from a hinge recess using a straight bit in a router. The bit is set to cut to the depth of the recess, and afterwards the corners can be finished off using a chisel.

Flush overlay doors Modern, adjustable **concealed hinges** are the most commonly used. There are many types available, and they come with full installation instructions. Some types are face-fitted and simply screw in place on the inside face of the door, but usually a special Forstner bit is used to drill a wide, flat-bottomed hole for the hinge body in the rear surface of the door. Next the base plate is screwed to the side frame. Finally, the hinge is attached to the base plate and the adjusting screws are turned until the door fits perfectly.

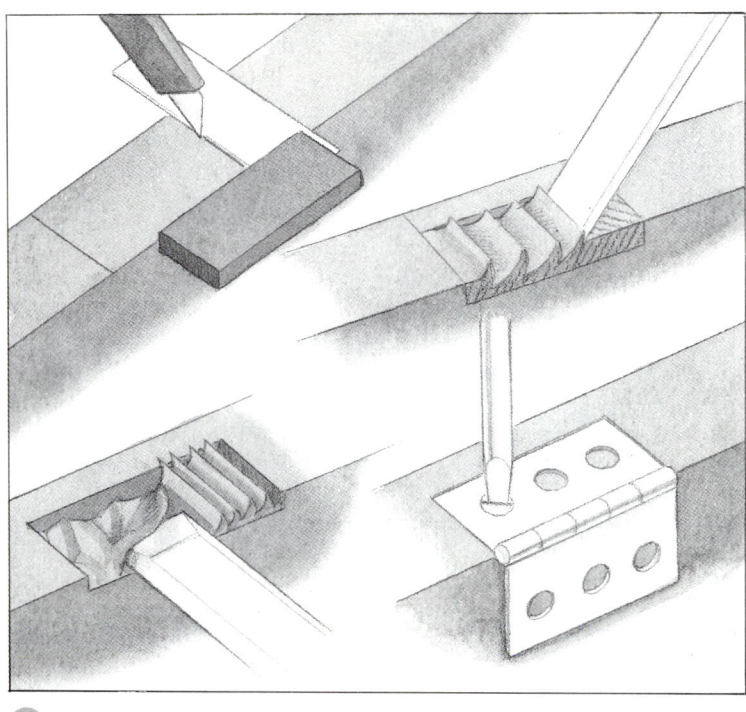

⑥ The Stages in Fitting a Butt Hinge
Using a try square and a utility knife, mark out the length of the hinge. With a marking gauge mark width and thickness of hinge flap. With chisel vertical, cut around outline of hinge. Make series of cuts across width of recess. Pare out the waste, then check that the flap lies flush. Once this is done, screw the butt hinge in place.

④ Fitting a Flush Hinge
Flush hinges are very easy to fit. Screw the outer flap to the frame and the inner flap to the door.

⑤ Fitting a Butt Hinge
Butt hinges must be recessed into the door frame so that hinge flaps are flush with the surface.

⑦ Fitting Face-fixed Concealed Hinges
This hinge is simply screwed to the inside face of the door and frame.

⑧ Fitting Recessed Concealed Hinges
Blind hole is drilled for hinge body. The base plate arm is adjustable.

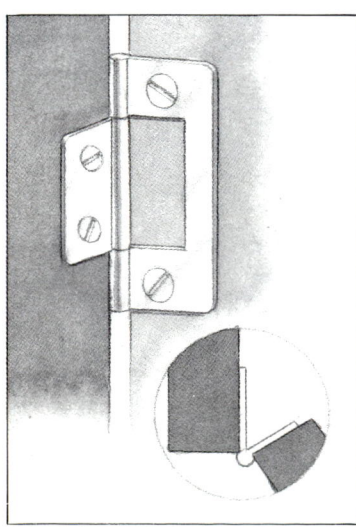
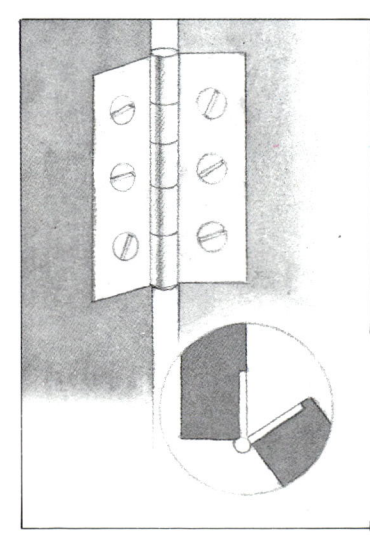
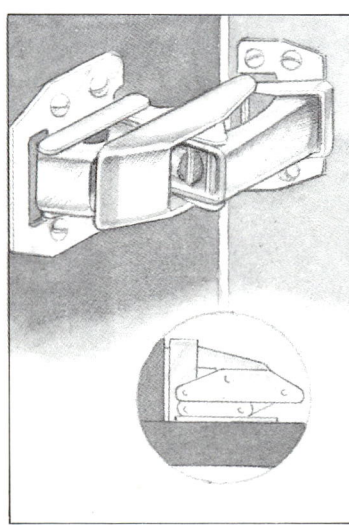
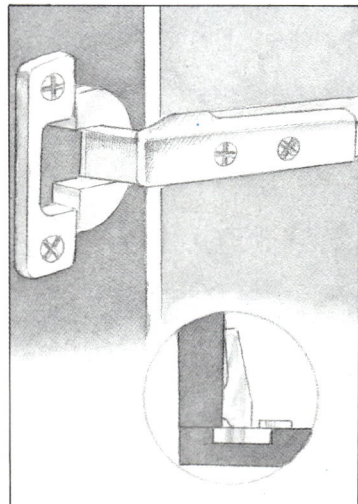

FITTING CATCHES

Many types of concealed hinges have built-in closers, so catches are not required. With conventional hinges, **magnetic catches** are popular. The magnet is fitted to the side of the cabinet and the catch plate is then positioned on the magnet. The door is closed on to the catch and pressed hard so that the catch plate marks the door. The door is opened and the catch plate is then simply screwed to the door.

Ball catches are very neat devices. On the central edge of the door a hole is drilled to accept the body of the ball catch, which is pressed into place. The door is closed and the ball marks the edge of the cupboard. The door is opened and the striker plate carefully positioned to coincide with the center of the ball. If you are recessing the striker plate, its outline should be drawn around, using a utility knife. The strike plate is then recessed into the cabinet so that it lies flush with the surface enabling the catch to operate smoothly.

FITTING DOOR LIFT MECHANISMS

Actual fitting instructions vary with the type of mechanism, but basically all screw inside the cupboard on the side of the frame, close to the top. Two lift mechanisms are required per door, and they are designed to throw the door upwards and outwards, and clear of the ceiling.

With the more sophisticated type (fig 4, left-hand illustration), the mechanism is screwed to the side face of the frame just below the top of the cupboard, and just inside the front edge. It is held with three screws. The lift-up flap is screwed to the opening part of the mechanism with two screws, the top screw being fixed down from the top edge of the flap by the thickness of the cupboard top plus $1\frac{1}{8}$in (28mm). This ensures that the flap opens without damaging the cupboard front or the ceiling.

FITTING LOCKS

The neatest lock is a **cabinet mortise lock**. To fit, mark the center line

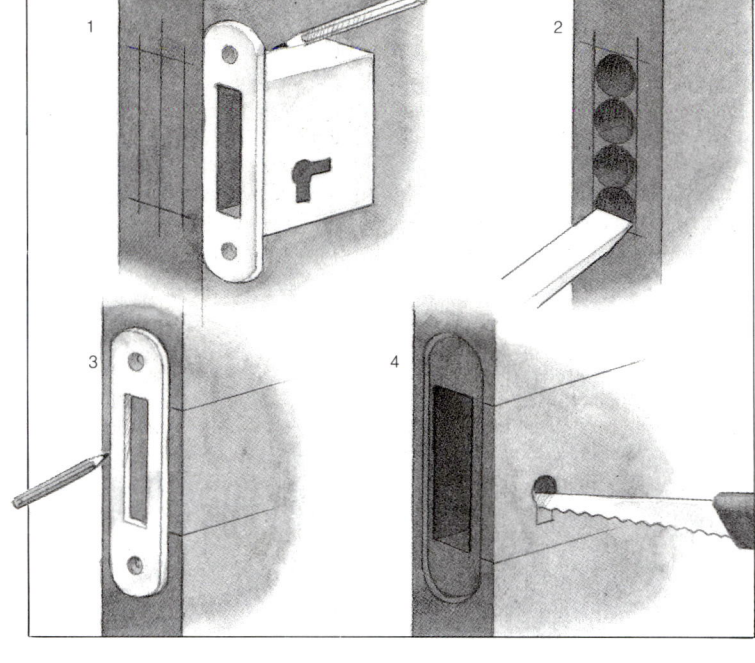

③ Fitting a Cabinet Mortise Lock to a Cupboard Door
1 Mark the center line on the door edge and measure and mark the width and thickness of lock on the door edge. *2* Use a brad-point bit to clear out mortise and clear out the slot with a chisel. *3* Push lock into mortise slot and mark around cover plate. *4* Cut recess for plate; form keyhole using compass saw.

① Magnetic Cupboard Catch
A magnetic catch is screwed to the inside face of a cabinet and the catch plate is screwed to the frame.

② Fitting a Ball Catch
Drill door edge centrally for ball catch body which is pressed in place. Striker plate fixes to frame.

④ Fitting Top-hinged Door Lift Mechanism
Two types of door lift mechanism are shown below. On the left is a combined hinge and stay, and on the right is a conventional stay. Both are designed to throw the door upwards and then to keep it held open.

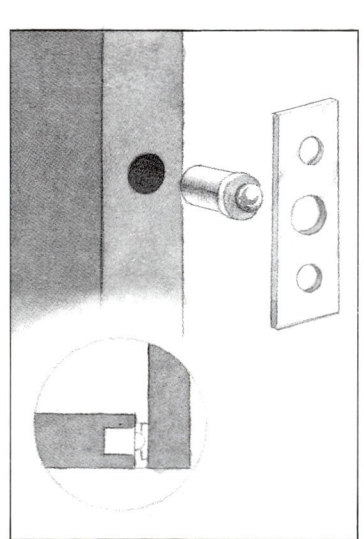

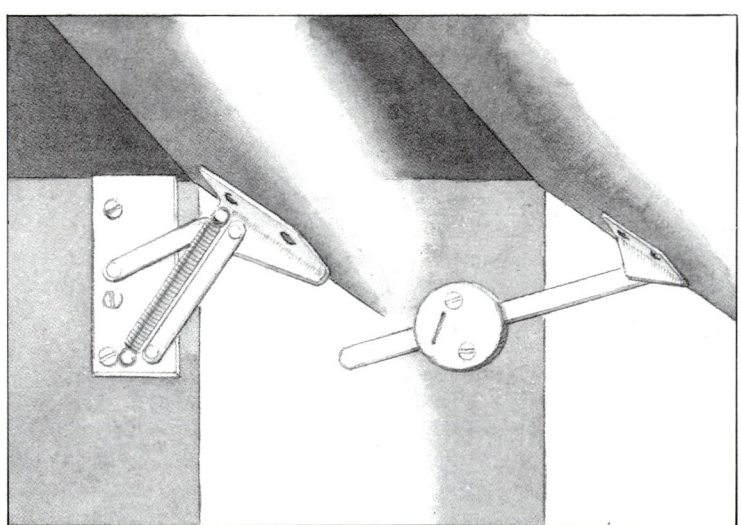